COFFEE
LUNCH
COFFEE
A PRACTICAL FIELD GUIDE FOR MASTER NETWORKING

I LOVE networking!

ALANA MULLER

NRC

ISBN-13: 978-0988347304 (Alana Muller Enterprises, LLC)

ISBN-10: 098834730X

Edited by Leigh Haber.

Cover and text design by Joann Bittel.

Dedication

To Marc and Ian.
Three is a magic number.

To my parents, Charlene and Max Muller.
You are my biggest fans; I am yours, too.

Acknowledgments

When I first began networking, I didn't set out to write a blog. Nor was a book a lifelong ambition. Rather, both became de facto as I sought a new professional reality and networking became the clear path to bring that to fruition. That the coffee-lunch-coffee approach worked for me helped me to understand that it could work for others, too.

Indeed, those others... many others, as it turned out, confirmed that coffee-lunch-coffee was a useful construct for anyone looking to connect with people. They lined up with me, propped me up and cheered me on to create this body of work. And, so, with that, I THANK YOU!

Thank you first to the Fab Five: Bob Grant, Howard Jacobson, Lesa Mitchell, Eric Morgenstern and Scott Slabotsky — when I decided to embark on my networking journey, you were my first five connections and you encouraged me to advance quickly toward my dreams. Special appreciation to my first networking buddies: Maria Stecklein Flynn and Scott Carson — your unselfish brand of support helped me to learn the true value of networking. I am grateful also to Tim Hannan who made me believe in the power of shared connections. And, I would be no where without the support of the 200 individuals who willingly took my calls and responded to my emails during the early days of building my network — you welcomed me into your networks and enabled me to create mine — you wrote this story.

It was Team Kansas City (Munro Richardson, Stephanie Guerin and Kelly Voitenko), as a result of Bob Miles' Genius of Warren Buffett course at the University of Nebraska at Omaha and several car rides to and fro, that actually lit the fire to get me to start writing.

Once I got going, my blog commentators and providers of many Facebook "likes" encouraged me to keep writing — especially Debby Barash, Jack Lerner, Michele Markey, Eric Muller, Shawn Muller, Kristin Schultz — many of whom are also contributors to this book and others who read early chapters and provided invaluable feedback.

Still others took time to serve as advisors, create exercises, provide resources and share specific recommendations during exclusive CLC interviews — for this I am especially grateful to Sunny Bates, Karen Cottengim, Tom Denham, Susan Freeman, Eric Morgenstern, Sara Nelson, Andrew Nemiccolo and Laurel Touby.

So many writers, entrepreneurs and thinkers contributed to this book, in a variety of ways. I have tried to credit them in every possible way, but let me also say thank you to everyone whose ideas helped inform this book—your words, your thoughts, your work has helped shape not only this book but also my entire networking philosophy. Additionally, many of my blog readers and networking contacts provided me with personal comments and insights — some of whose quotations you will read within — whether they actually appear, I so appreciate the remarks.

A huge THANK YOU to the official CLC team: My editor, Leigh Haber, is the real deal; her experience, insight and collaborative spirit helped to ensure *Coffee Lunch Coffee* was curated and organized in a way everyone could appreciate and utilize. My designer, Joann Bittel, possesses the perfect combination of creativity and expertise — she made sure we all had fun and didn't take this very serious work too seriously by infusing a touch of whimsy into our project. Ladies, I am so lucky to have found and had the opportunity to work with you both — I consider you not just my colleagues, but also my friends.

A special shout out to Ron Berg of Ron Berg Studio and Lindsey Patterson of Coffee Girls for a productive and fun photo shoot at a super cool location. And, thanks to Bryan Azorsky of Nodebud for creating a digital experience for *Coffee Lunch Coffee* of which any author would be proud.

To my grandparents, Rosie and Sidney Carr, thank you for your love and encouragement — I continue to appreciate your inquiries into my work and this very special project.

To my mom, Charlene Muller — thank you; even when few others understood what I was doing when I was taking all of those meetings way back when, you did. You encouraged me to keep going, to keep meeting people, to keep pursuing my goals. Then, when *Coffee Lunch Coffee* became more than a lifestyle, you were among my earliest blog supporters. You are my best friend, my mentor and guide. I am forever grateful.

To my dad and lifelong copy editor, Max Muller, a storied author and writer in his own right and the smartest human I know, a mere thank you is not enough. You promised you would stay up all night if you had to to make this writing (and all of my other essays since kindergarten) the best it could be, and you did. With every chapter that came off my laptop, you worked to make each better. As ever, Daddy Max gets an A+ from a very grateful and devoted admirer.

To my husband, Marc Hammer... when I returned from that trip to Chicago to tell you that I planned to leave my job to embark on something new, you didn't laugh or look confused or scared — you said, "YES!" You urged me on, you read every blog post before it became public, you encouraged me, you challenged me to do better, you continue to do all those things. You called this whole experiment an investment in our future. Thank you. You are my true partner and I love you.

To my son, Ian Alexander Hammer; you are my true inspiration. Your charisma and natural ability to build relationships is a wonder — we should all be so blessed. You make me so proud. I am a better person because of you and I love you so very much.

No doubt, I have inadvertently and mistakenly left off several very important people who I certainly did not intend to exclude from this set of acknowledgments. My sincere apologies. Please know, whether your name appears in the prior paragraphs, I am very grateful to so many people who have made such an important, positive and meaningful difference in my life. Thank you for your encouragement and support.

Note, this book is based on my own experiences with building a solid personal, professional network. It incorporates many of the writings that originally appeared in my blog, CoffeeLunchCoffee.com, some of them verbatim. If you are a reader of my blog and some of this looks familiar to you, it is likely because you have seen it before on the blog. You will discover, however, that this field guide enables you to take immediate action through exercises and recommendations that you will not have previously seen. You will also note that few outside research studies or papers are referenced; *Coffee Lunch Coffee* is largely based on my own personal experiences — call it "primary research" with a focus group of one. As time goes on, I intend to continue my networking journey. Please join me so that we may connect and become lifelong learners together.

— Alana Muller

Table of Contents

[INTRODUCTION]   [1]

[ONE]   Why Network? What is Your Purpose?   [15]

[TWO]   Prep Work   [27]

[THREE]   Changing It Up   [49]

[FOUR]   Time to Take the Plunge   [63]

[FIVE]   Your Networking Portfolio   [73]

[SIX]   Networking: People, Places, Things   [83]

[SEVEN]   Step Outside Your Comfort Zone   [97]

[EIGHT]   The Networking Master Class   [109]

[AFTERWORD]   [124]

Introduction

I love networking. And, so should you. ^[1]

Is there a question that networking is an essential tool for any professional, whether presently in or out of a job? No, of course not. Networking is something that in this economy is a necessity, not a luxury, at a time when businesses are fundamentally changing. These changes are often occasioned by seismic consequences for employees.

When it comes down to it, networking is really just a term for connecting with other people, about establishing community, about deepening one's sense of belonging. And if you are effectively networking, you are giving back as much as you are getting. You will find that networking offers something greater than the chance to get a hot tip on a new business opportunity.

If you've ever read my blog, CoffeeLunchCoffee.com, you already know that I love networking, though it may seem like an odd thing to love. After all, isn't netWORKING, well, work?? — something you do dutifully, when you have to look for a new job or find a new client?

But that's not the way I see it. For me, networking is like part of my DNA.

With few exceptions, I leave each networking encounter —
whether large event or one-on-one conversation — smarter than when
I arrived; and, with a new or renewed professional relationship that
typically pays dividends for years to come for all parties. However, that
doesn't mean networking isn't also hard work.

COFFEE-LUNCH-COFFEE-REPEAT

In seeking to improve my own networking skills, I began a blog in
November of 2011, CoffeeLunchCoffee.com, in which I share many of
my thoughts, observations, tips and advice on mastering the art (and
science) of networking.

The inspiration for *Coffee Lunch Coffee* can be traced all the way
back to November of 2007, when I decided to leave my job of 10 years
to find something new. Like many of you when faced with a major
change in life, whether that change was forced on you or it's voluntarily
undertaken, I had to plan my next move.

After months of planning and preparation, I was finally able to take
the plunge, to leave my comfortable corporate position. For the next nine
months, until I found a new position, I attended 160 meetings and met
200 new people, all through networking. During that time, I structured
my days around three main meetings: One in the morning (coffee), one
at midday (lunch), and one in the afternoon (coffee again) (though truth
be told, I am more of a Coca-Cola® drinker than a coffee drinker!).

The upshot of all of those efforts was that I found I was able to
develop and establish a rock solid network that led me to an amazing
variety of opportunities, culminating in what I do today. What do
I currently do? I'm President of Kauffman FastTrac®, a not-for-profit
educational organization that helps entrepreneurs start and grow
companies, originally created by the Ewing Marion Kauffman Foundation
(the foundation of entrepreneurship). I am also a civically active member
of the Kansas City community, where I live with my family.

I want to share what I've learned, to empower you to create a network — and a process for network building — so you can reap the same benefits that I've come to enjoy through my personal professional network.

Networking is part art, part science. It's about knowing how to start and carry on a conversation, and about remaining well-informed. It's about listening and about being responsive. It's about building self-confidence and contacts. At times, it is about wanting something from someone else, but it is also about being generous with your own information, contacts and resources. Networking is something you should be doing every day, not just when you "need" to. It's a muscle that requires regular exercise.

It's no accident that some of the most successful people in the world are some of the best networkers. A friend told me that she recently attended an event at a woman's home in New York City, at which Arianna Huffington spoke to 70 women about building her business, about the unique challenges women face, and about "having it all." (Apparently, a lively discussion ensued about whether that was possible and what it would look like.) At the end of the talk, Huffington gave out her personal email address to every single person in the room. All were struck by her accessibility, her generosity, and by the fact that though she is clearly one of the most influential people in the world, she hasn't rested on her laurels. Arianna Huffington hasn't lost sight of the value of making new connections.

One of the ultimate marketing masters of our time, online guru and bestselling author Seth Godin, is also one of my favorite commentators on the subject of "social networking." In a recent interview, he observed that networking should never just be about who collects the most business cards, Facebook friends or Twitter followers. He said: "Networking that matters is about helping people achieve their goals, reliably, and repeatedly, so that over time, they have an interest in helping you achieve your goals." I can't improve on that definition.

MAKE A COMMITMENT

There have been times — namely, when I have taken on full-time consulting assignments or when work is especially busy, that I have fallen down on my networking mission (e.g. to connect or reconnect with at least five to ten people each week). I am disappointed with myself every time that happens. Don't let that happen to you! You honestly never know what opportunities might emerge just from having a simple cup of coffee with someone. Realizing that is usually motivation enough for me. When I start to slack off on my networking routine, I get right back up on the horse and refocus my efforts on enhancing my relationship base. No matter how busy we are, it only takes a few minutes each day to make good on our promise to ourselves to spend regular, dedicated time connecting with people.

For those of you who need a job right now and are utilizing networking as your best tool for identifying your next opportunity, congratulations! You are already ahead of the game.

For those of you who are just starting your networking efforts, [4] I suggest you treat networking like a full-time job. By that I mean every day, get up, get dressed, and go to work! Don't plan to roll out of bed at 9 a.m. and wander into your home office in your pajamas to check on your emails or surf the web. You will have missed your opportunity since morning coffee meetings kick off no later than 7:30am or 8:30am.

Instead, set your alarm and get up early, take a shower, brush your teeth, shave, put on your make up, comb your hair, get dressed and whatever else it is that you do to get ready to go to a corporate job. Make yourself breakfast, and go for a run, or read the paper, or engage in any other ritual you might have done as part of your pre-work routine when you were commuting to the office, but plan accordingly since you are expected in the "office" early. And then, hit the street! Remind yourself that since you are your own boss, you need to be accountable for getting into work on time, (you wouldn't want to displease your boss, would you?) ready to be productive and to schedule and attend networking meetings. And, be sure to have your list of objectives for the day clearly in mind, or written out. I am a huge believer in to-do lists. They will absolutely help you stay organized and on message.

- *Establish a routine.* If it helps you to get started, write it down, starting with a 7 a.m. Wake Up! Also, know where you are going. If you have an office outside your home, go there. If not, come up with someplace else to call an office (e.g. the local coffee shop, the library, a hotel lobby with wi-fi).

- *If you are unemployed, remind yourself that networking is your full-time job, so own it.* Some people find it helpful to talk with a recruiter; others participate in local job clubs. Karen Cottengim, founder and career guide at TRUE NORTH Career Strategy, suggests a few other resources such as:

  ☐ **job-hunt.org** This website lists networking and job search support groups by state, plus 1,500 professional associations and societies by industry and a list of over 250 company, corporate, military and government alumni groups;

  ☐ **meetup.com** This is the world's largest network of grassroots groups. More than 9,000 groups get together in local communities each day, each one with the goal of improving themselves or their communities;

  ☐ **linkedin.com** LinkedIn enables members to connect with millions of other professionals and to join virtual industry and/or shared interest groups (more about this topic in Chapter Two);

  ☐ **toastmasters.org** This international organization helps individuals build public speaking skills and personal networks; and

  ☐ College alumni associations are also excellent resources for building personal networks.

[5]

- *Have a vision for what success might look like.* Using that vision, keep yourself on task by setting goals, both readily achievable ones, and ones requiring you to stretch. These should be daily, weekly and monthly in nature. Have an idea of how many people you would like to network with, who they are, what industries they come from, who you are going to ask for referrals, and when your next one-on-one encounter(s) should take place.

- *When someone in the neighborhood or in a social setting asks you what you do for a living, have a strong, clear answer ready,* e.g., "I am an attorney focused on social media and the law. In fact, I am currently looking for a great new opportunity. I would love to connect with firms and companies growing in this area. Would you be willing to meet me for coffee to discuss further? Here's my card." And have that card ready!

I BELONG

Earlier this year, I attended my tenth consecutive Berkshire Hathaway (BRK) annual shareholders' meeting in Omaha, co-hosted by Warren Buffett himself, as well as Charlie Munger, Vice Chairman of BRK.

As a shareholder, I was there to once again experience the "Oracle of Omaha" and his curmudgeonly, hilarious sidekick, Mr. Munger, as they responded to shareholder questions with their signature, charmingly informative brand of wisdom and wit. Since the arena at the CenturyLink Center could accommodate only 18,000 of us, we knew the remaining 19,000 unlucky shareholders would be relegated to nearby hotel ballrooms and convention center showroom floors where "overflow" viewing areas were established. That's why my husband, Marc, and I set our alarm for 4:30 that morning, getting to the event location by 5:15 a.m. so we could stand in line for premium seating until the doors officially opened. For the first time in years it wasn't raining the day of the show, but for the record, bad weather hadn't stopped us from standing in line those other years either.

When the witching hour of 7 a.m. finally arrived, we, like the thousands of other line standers, rushed the doors, run-walking while the security detail hollered "walk, don't run!" PHEW. We were in! The first order of business was to affix pre-made "Reserved" signs to our claimed seats with masking tape we'd brought along from home. After that, we made our way down to the floor to browse around "Berkyville," a Disney World-like pop-up city comprised of sophisticated, convention-style booths set up by some of the many Berkshire Hathaway-owned firms, e.g. Benjamin Moore® Paints, The Pampered Chef® Burlington Northern Santa Fe Railway® Clayton Homes®— you get the idea. We spent time at many of the company booths, grabbing a DQ® Dilly Bar® (at 7:15 a.m.), having our photo snapped with the GEICO Gecko® and the Fruit of the Loom® guys, and purchasing a big box of full-priced See's Candies® peanut brittle — yes, all BRK companies. Oh, and did

I mention that I purchased a pair of the Berkshire Hathaway, limited edition, Brooks® running shoes? Most comfy running shoes I've ever owned, or so it seems to me, though the truth is that I can't decide if they really are that comfortable or if how good they feel on my feet is due to what I call the "Berkshire Effect"... that is, my perception being positively and artificially skewed by my warm feelings of proudly belonging to the capitalist cult of BRK...? Yes, Brooks is also a BRK company.

All of these well-known, well-managed, successful, profitable firms belong to an elite group of companies hand-picked by the foremost portfolio manager in the world. Most of them are still run by third or fourth generation members of their founders' families. Uncle Warren (that's what I call him) leaves them to operate their companies as they see fit. Their only obligations to him involve continuing to manage the companies as if they hadn't been sold to BRK, i.e., providing monthly financials and engaging in regular succession planning, while thinking of Uncle Warren as their banker.

[7]

Though most of the CEOs are independently wealthy at this point — they continue to "work" for their firms — for BRK and for Warren Buffett — not because they have to, but because they want to. They enjoy being part of the family. They belong. Their ideas and opinions and thoughts matter, which gives them a sense of belonging. In fact, each year at the Annual Meeting, the opening video ends with a tribute to these managers — a song set to the tune of "My Favorite Things" from *The Sound of Music*, during which each manager's name and headshot scrolls across the screen as the lyrics exclaim, "Berkshire managers, they're the best for sure and to them we say, we love them, we thank them, we give them a bow 'cause they really make us proud!" Who wouldn't want to belong to that club?

Ah, **belonging**. I suppose it's that delicious sense of belonging that helps to explain why I engage in almost teenager-like behavior when it comes to this event, as if I am waiting to see my all-time favorite band.

It's crazy! It's ridiculous! It is lemming-like! And, yet, I've done it every year for the past 10 years, and I will do it next year, too. I'll be right back there, in that same arena, as long as our fearless [cult] leaders, Warren and Charlie, keep coming back to sit up there on the dais for five or so hours to answer questions from the press, from analysts and from shareholders. Hey, I'm not alone in my insanity. This year, there were 36,999 other acolytes too, among them Bill Gates and Bono. You see, we belong to the same group.

It's all about belonging. Seth Godin refers to this sensation as being part of a "tribe;" a subject he's devoted an entire book to. He says that it is human nature to need to belong — not just to one tribe, but to many tribes, whether religious, ethnic, economic, political, or arts related. Writes Godin in his book, entitled *Tribes*: "Human beings can't help it. We need to belong. One of the most powerful survival mechanisms is to be part of a tribe, to contribute to (and take from) a group of like-minded people."

The flip side, of course, is that awful, awkward feeling of NOT belonging. By way of example, when I first got to college, I was lonely. Sure, there was plenty of excitement, but I was 1,400 miles from home, knew next to nobody and wasn't quite sure where I fit in to that entirely new universe. I remember marveling at my roommate's ability to jump right into the fray. For instance, if we had both already gone to sleep, and a lively commotion started up in the hallway, no matter the time, my roommate would spring out of her bed and bolt through the door to join in the revelry. Meanwhile, I stayed self-consciously huddled under my covers. It seemed so easy for her. It took me many years to figure out her secret: That what she was doing was simply building relationships without getting too anxious about it; in other words, networking, albeit in the unique way that college students do, and having fun all the while.

My nine-year-old son does that. If he sees or hears "fun" going on… he joins right in as if he'd received a personalized, engraved invitation to be there... and he's the guest of honor! And everybody knows him. In his presence (or simply his aura), I have become "Ian's mom." He belongs. And others want to belong to him. He's already building a far-reaching social network that anyone would envy. Some folks just have it! That special something, a quiet charisma, that enables them to easily meet and build relationships with others. We all, however, are equipped to make this happen, irrespective of our personalities — extrovert or introvert.

From a business standpoint, as an intern at Hallmark® Cards in Kansas City during the summer of 1997, I witnessed firsthand a very powerful culture of belonging. Even back then, I laughingly called it the "cult of Hallmark." Everyone arrived at roughly the same time (right around 8 a.m. or earlier)... everyone broke for lunch around the same time (around noon or so)... from there, many of them (of **us**) went shopping at the discounted, in-house Hallmark store... and, then, at about 5 p.m., the parking lot cleared out. Empty. People who worked there, at least at the time that I did, loved it. They felt like they were part of a family. They belonged. I felt like I was part of that family... and I was there for only nine weeks one summer!

When I left Corporate America in 2008 to strike out on my own, one of my standard lines about the type of organization that I wanted to work with and for was one that "promoted a culture where I had a seat at the table." I was focused not so much on the amount of money that I would make, nor on the specifics of the work that I would do. Those things were important, certainly, but the characteristic that most interested me was whether I would like the culture, whether I would fit in, whether I would belong.

Belonging feels good. It bolsters confidence, pride and a sense of self. As we each engage in the practice of networking, we will be engaging in the practice of belonging. This, of course, does not mean that we will be forced to subsume our own identities. In order to belong, we don't have to hide or alter who we are; quite the contrary. Nor should we

[9]

feel that everyone we interact with should be just like us, or interested in exactly the same things. In fact, the more diverse one's social network, the richer and more robust the experience of networking will be, and the more it will enhance our lives.

Since I began networking in earnest, it has become a part of who I am — it is now part of my personal DNA. Now, I love "jumping in" to the social scene and getting to know others in all kinds of settings. But, as I mentioned previously, this did not always come easily for me. It took work. It took recognition that by putting myself out there, I would be more readily embraced by others. And, in so doing, I was able to build relationships, and a far-reaching network that continues to serve me well.

Before I set out on my own, I knew I had to prepare myself for that transition in terms of how I would next earn a living, where I would locate myself, and what sorts of people and types of companies I would spend that time with.

Where to start? Since I had defected from the group to which I had belonged for so long — that being Sprint® — I needed to discover a new way and place to belong. Instinctively, I understood that to discern my next step, I needed to get out there and talk to people. I needed to NETWORK! It was quickly, even painfully, obvious that I had been head down, overly (solely) focused on my insular, internal networking at Sprint, to the exclusion of all else. When it came down to it, I was left with few external professional contacts, something I knew I needed to turn around right away.

I discovered that once I began networking intentionally it was more difficult to stop than to keep on building. Once my network began taking shape, I started hearing the same names again and again. In fact, people started suggesting me as a great networking contact to others. Dots began connecting, I found my groove. I now happily and comfortably belonged to the professional community at large.

IT CAN CHANGE YOUR LIFE

My Coffee-Lunch-Coffee approach to networking has had a profound impact on my life — both personally and professionally. I'm sharing this approach with you in an effort to help you benefit from its principles.

Please know that you do have the potential to become a master networker. But why engage in this practice at all? The best networkers connect with others for long-term relationship building without knowledge of what, specifically, that relationship may ultimately bring to their lives. They do so in a completely selfless manner, without expectation of payback or remuneration. They are not networking simply to get ahead, or to change jobs, or to develop their sales pipeline. Rather, they are passionate about something, they want to connect and share their interests with others who are equally passionate. It is a virtuous cycle that can have major, long-term, life altering implications.

The question is, are you ready? How do you feel about networking? Are you energized by the prospect of meeting new people? Or does the very notion send you into fits of panic? Would you characterize yourself as an active networker? Or, are you unsure of where to begin, concerned that you might be asking too much of others? At times, it may feel intimidating, stressful or awkward. But now is the time to sharpen your networking skills, utilize this powerful tool and connect with others.

Whether you are in the throes of a career transition, a student with professional aspirations, a sales executive building your business, a current or potential entrepreneur seeking to grow or startup a company, an established doctor, lawyer, architect, CPA or other professional simply trying to connect or a community volunteer set on making a world of difference, I believe we must all, without fail, embrace networking and make it part of who we are. Networking plays a critical — perhaps THE most critical role — in determining our career paths, our level of success in business, how we are perceived in the community, how equipped we are to get things done.

What's in the box?
(Post from Seth Godin, July 21, 2012, sethgodin.com)

We hesitate.

We stall or try for perfect or have meetings or polish or avoid the final 'go' because we're afraid that it might not work, that the art won't be well received, that people will hate it.

Here's the thing: there's a box on the table. And you need to decide whether or not you're going to open it. All the wishing and planning and imagining isn't going to change what's already in the box. The act of opening it doesn't deserve anxiety because the contents of the box were determined a long time ago. What's in the box is in the box, regardless of how much anxiety goes into opening it.

Sure, do a great job, the best job you can do with the resources you've got. But then quit imagining and go ahead and open the box.

What this book is… a big nod to Networking, coupled with (not-so-)subtle winks at Leadership and Entrepreneurship. My hope is that you can digest these words in just a few sittings, and that they will ease any concerns or fears that you might have about the process. This book is meant to serve as a practical guide that you can review very quickly and put in practice immediately.

What this book is NOT, however, is a quantitative, statistically-based dissertation drawn from academic research. Rather, it is filled with tips, tricks and tools that I picked up through my own experience. The research, so to speak, is primary research of which my own experiences are the subject. In reading this book, along with new information, you may, if you are an active reader of my blog, recognize some of the most important lessons I have previously shared on CoffeeLunchCoffee.com.

And as you will read, I've also incorporated a few select stories from some of the foremost networking masters I have encountered along the way, either in real life, or through their books, speeches or other writings.

Coffee Lunch Coffee comprises a field guide designed to help you overcome your fears, surmount obstacles, gather courage and harness opportunities. It should spark a new energy, motivate you to get out there and ignite your desire to build community. Over the years, I hope it will serve as a long-term resource to refer back to when you need a networking boost.

So, grab a pencil, a cup 'o Joe and start writing in the margins. In the pages that follow are techniques to help you come up with a process of your own to build your network, enhance your leadership skills and begin to think entrepreneurially about your own life. Let's get started.

EXERCISE

[i.a] So, where do you fit in?

What type of culture or tribe resonates with you? Can you readily articulate the traits of a place, of an organization, of a group to which you do or would like to belong? As you continue your networking journey, think about your affiliations — or affiliations that you would like to make. In both scenarios, you will find rich ground for networking. Think first of WHAT it is you would like to affiliate with, then consider WHO is part of that experience with whom you can connect. Go on… join 'em!

To which Culture or Tribe do I want to belong?	Who do I know that already belongs?
Example: A local non-profit organization	*Example: Barry Alexander (who sits on the board of directors for the non-profit)*

ONE

WHY NETWORK?
WHAT IS YOUR PURPOSE?

Fear. Anticipation. Economic pressures. Confidence. Self-doubt. Resolve. Those were just some of the emotions roiling through me when I decided to leave my safe, secure executive job all those years ago. Like a parachutist I asked myself more than once, "Why jump out of a perfectly good airplane?"

I jumped voluntarily. Some of you are considering networking because you were pushed out of the plane. There was nothing voluntary about it.

Does it matter what brought you to this moment in time? Not really, because networking will help you overcome whatever challenges you are facing or goals you wish to achieve.

Establishing and maintaining your networking skills is crucial in terms of staying well-informed, connecting with new people who are relevant to your field, and keeping your name out there. As Daniel Pink observes in his classic book, *Free Agent Nation*, "…your network is your safety net. The vaster it is and the tighter its connections, the more likely you'll be able to survive."

Reid Hoffman, founder of LinkedIn and author of the bestselling book *The Start-Up of You*, also has some valuable insights on why maintaining a professional network today is absolutely essential. Perhaps the central and most profound observation he makes is that because the trajectory and substance of the typical career has changed so dramatically, from being akin to an "escalator," on which an employee constantly ascends over time, to being something far less linear and predictable, we must all think and act "like you're running a startup." The startup being you and your career. Looking at it from this perspective, you can easily see how fundamental maintaining a network is over the course of your life.

A NETWORK IS LIKE AN ECOSYSTEM

[18]

When the word "network" was first coined, it referred to systems of waterways, roads and other components of infrastructure that helped connect people and resources. When you think of the kind of networking we are discussing, you can visualize our professional networks as performing a similar function, that is, providing the support, resources, energy, and connectivity that enable us to engage with individuals, with our communities, with our industries, and with the larger world. When we think of networks that way we can appreciate the beauty and the necessity of our mutual interdependence.

A network is a kind of ecosystem. It's organic. It's dynamic. Ecosystems are defined by the network of interactions among a community of living organisms (e.g. people, plants, animals, insects, microorganisms, etc.) along with the non-living elements of their environment (e.g. air, water, and mineral soil), all working together as one, large, interdependent, living system. Well, our own familial, professional and social networks function like ecosystems. Ecosystems operate best in a state of equilibrium.

But disturbances are inevitable — so is change. In the ecosystem that makes up our universe, changes are sometimes human-made, while others are the product of natural forces. Sometimes changes come in the form of relatively minor events. Sometimes as catastrophes. When an ecosystem is rocked by change it must adjust and find a new equilibrium. It must find a new way of operating that still enables all of its systems to function, even under very different circumstances.

For most professionals in the last half of the twentieth century, profound changes were few, as far as their industries and jobs were concerned. There was a certain way things happened. You know, we graduated from high school and many of us then went to college. If we didn't go to college, we entered a trade or industry, worked for the same company for many years, perhaps until retirement.

Similarly, if we did go to college, after graduation, a predictable journey continued. We entered a profession and moved steadily up "the ladder of success." We received regular salary increases and promotions, perhaps even bonuses. We largely felt secure in the knowledge that even if we lost our jobs, other, similar positions were abundant, so we wouldn't be out of work for long; and when we returned, we would do so at a comparable or higher rate of pay. Because we were experts at our jobs, we could see what was coming around the corner. We could count on things remaining largely as they were. Nice. Safe. Secure. You could almost hear birds singing in the background…

As we look back at that period from our present vantage point, that time almost seems quaint — a sort of rosy bubble, a tranquil, prosperous and privileged span of time. Since then, there have been numerous "disruptions" to professional ecosystems. Technological advances have had the effect of eliminating the need for many jobs, while others have been outsourced to cheaper labor markets. The internet has been another source of disruption. Globalization, economic regulation and deregulation, workers living longer and putting off retirement —

these factors and many others have come together to uproot and fundamentally transform entire industries, which in turn has resulted in contraction of those industries, and in the failure or down-sizing of many companies. The result is that professional security is all but non-existent and, now more than ever before, one's personal professional network is more valuable and critical to build and maintain.

Change is frightening, especially if it is forced on you, but I feel great optimism. There is no doubt that individuals, families and entire communities are feeling the pain. And, yes, the professional world is still competitive, especially as more people vie for fewer and fewer well-paid, full-time positions. However, there is that other side of the coin. We are slowly beginning to realize that it isn't over for us if we are not occupying executive level positions within large corporations. On the contrary. Entrepreneurship is the watchword. Startups abound — in fact, as of March 2012, according to Kauffman Foundation research, new

companies are formed at a rate of about 543,000 per month in the United States alone.

As we look for new ways to think about work and how to own our own destinies, people are finding within themselves resources they never knew they had. And they are discovering that, whereas the previous professional era was about secrecy, competition, and company loyalty, in today's marketplace, it is transparency, cooperation, and "rolodex loyalty," or **networking**, that produce success.

The professional ecosystem that was so profoundly disrupted by a perfect storm of factors is finding a new equilibrium, and to survive within it, it is paramount that we depend on a very different network, one that consists of people we know or come to know, and who know us. If our own individual ecosystem experiences a cataclysmic event, such as being laid off or fired, or losing a major client, we can't just wait for the fates to restore the natural order. Instead, we must be able to quickly recalibrate, to assess what resources remain at our disposal —

what our strengths are — to quickly pivot, and deploy those resources in the most effective way. How can networking help? If we are supported by a living, breathing network that we have carefully tended over time, it is much easier to land on our feet during those times, to achieve a new equilibrium. Having that network underneath us is like having a safety net, something that reassures us every day that if the worst happens we have something to fall back on.

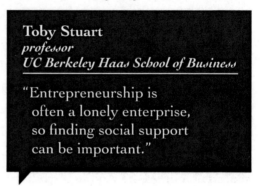

Toby Stuart
professor
UC Berkeley Haas School of Business

"Entrepreneurship is often a lonely enterprise, so finding social support can be important."

One of the beauties of having a network to tap, one that you've nurtured over time, is that it's there when you need to make a change, for whatever reason. But if you're reading these words and thinking: "I have a job I love and I don't plan on ever leaving it, so why do I need to be concerned about building and maintaining a network?" for me the answer is threefold.

[19]

In the first place, let's face it — you never know. Things happen. Your company could be sold, there could be a change in administration that doesn't favor you, your position could be altered in ways that cause you to be dissatisfied or, dare I say it, you may get bored and find yourself longing for something different. If the unexpected happens, and you find yourself needing to find something new, you don't want to have to expend valuable time you could be using to pursue solid job leads building a network you didn't anticipate having to lean on. What's my point? It's simple — even if you are presently happily employed, start building your network now, today and not tomorrow when you suddenly need it.

Secondly, most industries in the world today are undergoing major sea changes; rapid, fundamental transformations that make it difficult for most of us to keep up and stay clued in. Therefore, it's vital that we keep our ears to the ground just to keep up with how these changes are impacting our industries, our companies and our jobs. Networking affords us the chance to do that. It helps keep us on the leading edge instead of behind the curve.

And third, and perhaps most importantly, networking prevents us from getting too insular, too self-focused, and encourages us to think about how and why we are connecting with others. Ask yourself: Are you being generous with your thoughts and ideas? Is there information that you've learned that can be shared to benefit your colleagues? Are you doing a good enough job of building a constellation of mentors, colleagues, supporters who depend on you, and on whom you can depend? Many believe that we are evolving as a global culture in ways that make "dog-eat-dog" competition and zero-sum games ("I win, you lose") less important, and compassion and cooperation more essential. Are you contributing to the compassion and cooperation quotient? And in a work world in which it is no longer the corporation that is the center of most professional lives, but networks, are you ensuring that you are a fully contributing member to those networks?

On a practical, daily level, there are some excellent reasons to regularly, consistently network. Here are just a few:

1. **From the point of view of finding a new position**, according to a Cornell University 2011-2012 Career Services Guide, **it is estimated that networking plays a role in up to 75 percent of hiring decisions**. I know! That's an unbelievably high percentage. It's increasingly true that it's "who you know," not just what's on your résumé. Fortunately, social media resources such as LinkedIn, Facebook, Twitter, etc. make it possible to jump-start the networking process.

2. **Networking opens doors**. First you access the people you know best. Those people then make other introductions for you, and soon you will find yourself in conversations with a growing group of influencers, with people who are the deciders when it comes to who to hire and where to invest money, the people who really make things happen. Who doesn't want access to that universe?

3. **Networking requires that you be meeting-oriented, that you set up face-to-face appointments, which is how meaningful connections happen.** Using your résumé, email contact, and phone to get the appointment is one approach, but face time is the Holy Grail.

4. **Networking teaches you to be adaptable.** Although the Bureau of Labor Statistics does not track how often Americans change jobs, all sorts of articles and commentary related to jobs note job changes ranging from 7 to 10 times over the span of a career. What is the right number? I don't know. What I do know is that it is rare these days for anyone to stay in the same job, or even in the same company, for their entire career. Networking keeps you from getting rusty. Rust keeps you from moving freely — or moving at all.

5. **Networking is an energy boost.** Meeting new people, preparing yourself for your next meeting, doing your homework, practicing your conversational skills — these all keep you fresh and on your game.

When I first set out to start my own venture, I focused entirely on networking. It wasn't long before others noticed what I was up to and began making comments like "I met someone yesterday who knows you." Almost invariably, that "someone" was a person I'd met via networking. It was awesome. I loved getting those comments, and compliments, such as "you know everyone" or "everyone knows you!" Of course, neither is literally true, but it had become directionally correct within my circle, within my community. To this day, I still love it when people observe, "Wow! You are really well connected." It means that I have access to an important asset, an important group of people I can tap for the right reasons at any time. And it means that I have a sense of belonging that is not solely connected to the wonderful company I head now. I belong to a network I had a hand in building, which will continue to exist whatever I am doing professionally in the future as long as I continue to tend it.

Danny Freeman
entrepreneur

" I think that one of the greatest misconceptions about networking is that it should be challenging at all. It should be fun! Those who view the process as 'work' are often those who have the most trouble and least success in the process. When I personally realized that each and every person I connect with has a unique perspective and experience to bring to the table, the process became so much less of a challenge and more of an exciting activity.

" If you imagine that everyone is pursuing their unique versions of an ideal life, they've acquired lessons and experiences towards that unique pursuit on a completely different path from the one that you might be on. The person who can step back and empathize with others' varying situations and interpret the subliminal lessons from their contacts' diverse viewpoints will ultimately be the most powerful and effective networker."

In November 2011, I hosted the Kauffman FastTrac® Global Women's Summit — a day for entrepreneurially minded women to come together in a collaborative learning environment. Though it was unintentional (albeit, perhaps, not that surprising), the overarching theme of the event turned out to be NETWORK, NETWORK, NETWORK. As an example, from a panel called "Financing and Fundraising for Your Company," here is an excerpt from what the panelists had to say:

- "It's important to build a narrative for your business. Go in knowing what you must say about your endeavors to capture the interest of the other party."
  Eric Jackson, CEO and Co-Founder, CapLinked

- "When interacting (with networking contacts), passion, honesty, and authenticity are critical."
  Alexis de Raadt St. James, Founder and Chairman, The Althea Foundation

- "One coffee meeting is not enough to build a relationship. Make it a stepping stone to get to the next meeting." *Greg Gottesman, Managing Director, Madrona Venture Group*

So I ask you:

- **Would you call yourself well-networked?**

  - I know many people in my own city, industry and/or interest groups.
    ☐ Yes   ☐ No

  - Those people know me, too.
    ☐ Yes   ☐ No

  - I find it easy to meet new people, gather information and seek to connect others.
    ☐ Yes   ☐ No

- **If not, what would it take you to get there?**

- **How many contacts or touch points would you need to move in this direction?**

In the exercise at the end of this chapter is a simple worksheet structure you can use to begin keeping track of the networking connections that you make.

IDENTIFY YOUR PURPOSE

"Wake up every day knowing the one or two people who you must talk with. Put it on your list of action items for the day. Do not rest until you connect with them." *Jean Case, CEO, The Case Foundation*

As important as the basic tools of effective networking are, it is at least as vital that we know what our purpose is. This is where we begin to realize that the best networkers are the ones who are not only chasing down people and information who can directly help them, but who live their lives with clarity of intention, and who reflect that clarity in everything they do.

> **Frank Bonura**
> *"The Connecter" and Executive Agent*
>
> "Networking is simply an army of people waving your banner."

Personally, I don't feel I have only one purpose in life. I bet you don't either.

I know that I seek to be the best mother, wife, and daughter possible, and to enrich the lives of my family and friends, whom I love deeply. As the leader of an organization, I aim to guide Kauffman FastTrac® to financial success, while ensuring that my team members have fulfilling, meaningful professional experiences. For our customers, my hope is that our products and services help them in their quest to grow economies and improve lives on a global scale. In the community, I aim to give back in a way that "teaches a man to fish," and leaves the world a little bit better off. And for my readers, I am intent on helping you on your professional journey by sharing information, insights and experiences that I have personally benefited from through my networking efforts.

One of my favorite quotations on "purpose" was written by Jon Kabat-Zinn, in his book *Wherever You Go, There You Are*. I realize it's a little esoteric, but I think you will take from it as much as I do:

> *"If what happens now does influence what happens next, then doesn't it make sense to look around a bit from time to time so that you are more in touch with what is happening now, so that you can take your inner and outer bearings and perceive with clarity the path that you are actually on and the direction in which you are going? If you do so, maybe you will be in a better position to chart a course for yourself that is truer to your inner being."*

So I ask you: What's your purpose? Do you know where to look, where to find it? Take a moment to write down a few thoughts. Don't try to organize your list. Just write down whatever first comes to your mind. If you're stumped, ask your spouse or partner, or your mother, a best friend, a colleague. Ask them what it is that you bring to their lives. Ask yourself what gifts you have to share with the world that you should be capitalizing on personally and professionally. Be prepared to talk with your networking contacts about your purpose, and ask them about theirs. Be sure that you are engaging in meaningful conversations through networking that will propel you and your contacts forward on your respective paths.

I'm going to help you find your purpose by offering some brain teasers and other exercises in the chapters that follow; however, before I do, let me direct you to the words of Tony Hsieh, CEO of the wildly successful online company, Zappos.com. In his book *Delivering Happiness: A Path to Profits, Passion, and Purpose,* he discusses how he and his team created a list of ten core values, which they continue to use in making hiring decisions, and setting company objectives. While Zappos devised this list to steer an entire company in its evolution, I think his formula works for the individual as well. Here are the core values Zappos came up with. Read it and use it to reflect on YOUR own core values.

[25]

1. Deliver WOW Through Service
2. Embrace and Drive Change
3. Create Fun and a Little Weirdness
4. Be Adventurous, Creative, and Open-Minded
5. Pursue Growth and Learning
6. Build Open and Honest Relationships with Communication
7. Build a Positive Team and Family Spirit
8. Do More with Less
9. Be Passionate and Determined
10. Be Humble

What are your core values? In chapter two, we will create a series of lists, the last of which is called "Non-Negotiables." Non-negotiables are built on a foundation of core values. As you move on to chapter two, start thinking about what is important to you. Be sure to consider your life at home, at work and in the community.

EXERCISE

[1.a] Networking Contacts Database

My approach to managing my contact database was through the use of a Microsoft® Excel spreadsheet. You may have another method of contact management — perhaps a CRM software package or the like. Whatever the case, be sure to keep it up to date so that it can be used as tool to help you maintain your network with complete information.

The fields that I tracked in my spreadsheet included:

- First Name
- Last Name

- Company

- Title

- Address (Street, City, State, Zip Code)

- Direct Office Phone

- General Office Phone/Switchboard

- Mobile Phone

- Email

- Referred By

- Meeting Date 1

- Notes from Meeting 1

- Etc.

To download a copy of my template, visit CoffeeLunchCoffee.com.

[TWO]

PREP WORK

A friend recently asked me how I would respond to the following question: "I need to make a professional change, but I'm not sure what my options are, and I feel overwhelmed when I think about getting out there to network. What do you advise?"

I told her I would probably start by changing the question itself. I suggested that she substitute the following, less daunting question: "I am considering what my professional options are and see networking as a first step. How do you suggest I systematically begin?"

How should you begin? Well, it's simple. Start with that sage piece of advice we've all heard, namely: "Always eat that elephant one bite at a time." No need to gobble it down all at once! In other words, take a breath — in fact, breathe deeply, and take a few breaths — inner calm is essential to orderly change, or to taking on a new challenge. Pace yourself. There is no need to feel overwhelmed and intimidated. In fact, networking helps you to break down "change" by divvying it up into a series of appointments, meetings and connections, so that you are gradually, thoughtfully, opening your eyes (and your brain and heart) to all that is out there. That is essential to preparedness.

Even before you sit down to figure out who you will reach out to, first, as you begin the networking process, consider this advice from Tom Peters:

You are your product — develop it.

Find a mirror. Stand in front of it.

Smiling,

Saying… 'Thank you.'

Doing… jumping jacks (or some equivalent thereof)

For God's sake, WHY?, you ask.

Smiling begets a warmer environment.

Thanking begets an environment of mutual appreciation.

Enthusiasm (the likes of those jumping jacks) begets enthusiasm…

How do you motivate others?

Answer: motivate yourself first.

—From *The Little BIG Things: 165 Ways to Pursue Excellence*

Why is this so inspiring? First, Tom Peters has been on a "search for excellence" for decades, and has professionally achieved it again and again. Yet, he doesn't stop trying to learn and to disseminate what he's learned. He also recognizes that there are some small, basic things that if done every day, routinely, can help us master what we are doing. Getting up earlier. Making funny faces at ourselves in the mirror to stay positive. Regularly exercising. (In his book *The Little BIG Things*, which is always good for inspiration, he cites the astonishment of a top business executive turned fitness trainer, who still finds it amazing that her fellow trainers all seem to be generally happier, more optimistic people than the rest of the population, simply because they take good care of their bodies, which produce those natural happy pills, a.k.a. endorphins.)

The point I'm making is that part of your game plan for networking mastery entails getting yourself into great shape, internally and externally, so that when you do sit down at your first meeting, you are exuding confidence, optimism, and a sense of being comfortable in your own skin. And while it's true that for some it's as if they were born this way, if you're not one of those lucky folks, with preparation, not to mention a little "fake it 'til you make it" chutzpah, you can learn to be as good at networking interactions as any "natural."

[29]

EXERCISE

[2.a] Mind ~ Body ~ Spirit

To prepare yourself for your networking journey, it can be useful to engage in a few visualization exercises to help you get into the right frame of mind. Susan S. Freeman, Executive Success Strategist and author of the book, *Step Up Now: 21 Powerful Principles for People Who Influence Others*, suggests the following actions:

1. **Mind.** Begin with the end in sight. Close your eyes. Envision a result that would be satisfying to you and that would create a win-win for both you and your contact. Get clear on what that is before you meet up. Do your homework on the person's background, interests and hobbies so you have grounds for connecting with them in a way that feels authentic.

2. **Body.** Prepare your emotions and moods for a successful outcome. Consider the following:
   a. What mood will serve you best for this conversation?
   b. What emotions will serve you best for this conversation?
   c. What will it take for you to feel those moods and emotions?

   Visualize yourself in the conversation; "feel" those moods and emotions strongly so they resonate throughout your body. Prepare in advance so you are sure to be ready when you are with your contacts.

3. **Spirit.** Sit quietly with your spine upright, with all the vertebrae stacked neatly one on top of the others. Make sure your feet are planted firmly on the floor. Drop your arms to your side. Roll your neck and shoulders to release any tension. Take a slow, long inhalation from your belly. You can even place your hand on top of your belly to make sure that on the inhale your belly extends outward, and on the exhale your belly contracts. If not you are breathing from the top of your lungs and not your belly. This is important because top of lung breathing promotes fear and anxiety; not a calm, centered presence. As you breathe in and out through the belly with long, slow deep inhalations, ponder the question of your care. What do you truly care about? How can you communicate that in today's networking session? How do you want to behave, carry yourself and speak? What do you want to make sure to cover in the conversation? Continue breathing like this for 3-5 minutes in the morning prior to the meeting. Visualize yourself there with this calm, centered breathing presence. When you feel complete, you may open your eyes. Know that you have prepared your mind, body, and spirit for connection and effective communication. This alone will help make networking enjoyable and effective.

Like exercising and eating right, networking is for life! There is no rush to complete a particular task. Rather, in networking, it is critically important to just get started, and to make a commitment to stick with it.

Be disciplined in your approach to networking. There will certainly be ebbs and flows in terms of the volume and quality of one's points of contact, but a true networker takes the long view, and sets a plan for building and maintaining a solid network that he or she will continue to build and maintain… forever.

To begin, pick just one contact. Take action by calling or emailing that individual to schedule a networking interaction, like coffee or lunch. Promise yourself that once that meeting is scheduled, and after it has taken place, you will take the appropriate follow-up actions, e.g.:

1. Send a confirmation email the day before reminding your target of your upcoming meeting. Be sure to include date, time, location and your own contact information.

2. Immediately following the meeting, send a thank you note and complete any tasks or next steps you discussed. (Note: I keep personalized stationary in my car and write my notes as soon as I leave the meeting and mail them off ASAP.) To be sure you remember what those next steps are; make a note of them on your calendar or in your journal.

3. Select your next contact and take action to set up an appointment with them. Repeat.

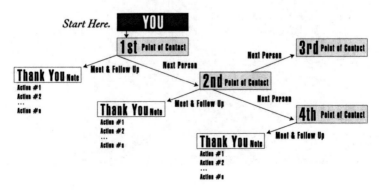

4. In addition to sending your contact a thank-you note, other follow-up actions could include sending a link or a copy of an article you discussed; following up with any contacts offered by that first point of contact, perhaps even circling back with contact #1 after you've heard from contact #2 to report back; scheduling another meeting with contact #1, etc.

A common question that often arises is whether you should know exactly what your "ask" is when you are about to begin scheduling appointments with new contacts, or reconnecting with old ones. The answer is that networking is an iterative process. What may be meaningful, important, and useful to you (or for that matter, to your contact) today, may be different from what you want or need later. Therefore, perfect clarity on this point is not a requirement. Having said that, it is extremely useful to set some goals, to know what you hope to accomplish through networking, so that you can prioritize the specific people or particular

[32]

Neal Schwartz
Vice President, Cerner Corporation

"The power of a network is critically important for those who are seeking to gain something… but what is most important is to remember to GIVE something back to the people that I'm connected with. It comes down to having a clear understanding of what role you intend to have as part of the connection. At times, I think that many people that are attempting to 'network' make a point to interact with someone with an inherent personal goal in mind of accumulating / collecting something for their own gain without the notion that it's important to GIVE. I have personally had to step back at times in the midst of discussions and qualify my role in the dialog. Am I serving as a mentor? A mentee? A listener? A confidant? What? I've found that the most meaningful connections that I've made are the instances where there is bi-directional benefit versus something one-sided."

types of people you want to connect with immediately; and, so you will be prepared for the question: "So what can I help you with?"

One of my favorite all-time quotes about networking comes from the founder and chairman of Business Network International, Ivan Misner, who's also written an excellent book on the subject. Here is the quote, and I urge you to type it up, print it out, and tape it to your computer screen: "Networking is about farming, not hunting."

What does he mean? Well, as we've discussed, networking is not just about getting in touch with people who can do something for you. In fact, if that is your approach, it will not work, certainly not in the long term. You have to be willing to invest in relationships before your contacts can be expected to trust you enough to put their own resources and credibility on the line for you. Although you need to create a wide and diverse network, filled with people at all levels of experience, and from different industries and areas of the community, you must value quality over quantity. It's not just about the width of your network, it's also about how deep those relationships go. Depth requires time, multiple encounters, thoughtfulness, and a slow maturation of mutual trust.

As you reach out to establish and maintain your network, it is useful to think about the fact that it is not just the people at the top you want to be reaching for — rather, from an organizational hierarchy perspective, it is important to reach out side-to-side and down, as well. A network that is made up of people of all ages, from all levels of business, and from a variety of industries and communities, is not only a way of warding off insularity and keeping on top of the latest developments, but it also means that you are meeting a range of interesting people, and that's half the fun of networking. The networking I've done over the course of my career has not only helped me professionally. Networking has also been the source of many of my closest friendships. You never know who the next big connector or influencer will be — it may not be the person you originally anticipated.

I've already said this but it bears repeating: While networking can help you achieve your goals in a timely fashion, it is important to remember that networking is about long-term relationship building versus short-term, one-time benefit. Those who network for the long-term without expectation of immediate remuneration of any kind will reap bigger rewards from networking interactions over time. And in the immortal words of master butcher and amateur philosopher, John Bichelmeyer, whose daughter's book-length tribute to her father's wisdom is a small masterpiece: "Don't act like it's your due. Take every chance to say thank you" (from *Lunchmeat & Life Lessons*, by Mary B. Lucas).

IDENTIFY YOUR IMMEDIATE NETWORKING GOALS. WHY DO YOU WANT TO CONNECT WITH OTHERS TODAY?

a. _____

_____

_____

b. _____

_____

_____

c. _____

_____

As to your goals — if you're currently in a position you are happy with, you may not be sure what your networking goals are. And if you are seeking something new, you may feel stumped as to what you want next and need some help with clarification. I find this list of ten steps toward goal clarification to be very helpful:

1. **Formulate a personal mission statement**. It can be one or two lines, or a whole essay, but take the time to sit down and put it on paper.

2. **Make four lists** (you will have the opportunity to do this at the end of the chapter):

a. *People you know in the community.*

When I sat down to assemble my first list, it was comprised of people with whom I had participated in community service initiatives, friends of mine with whom I had previously interacted only socially, people I knew through synagogue (church, temple or mosque for many of you!), parents of my son's school friends and sporting club teammates, and the like. Everyone on the list was a professional who I admired and who, I believed, would be supportive as I began the process of networking. Go back to your goals; think about who you know that may be able to help you achieve your goals.

b. *People who you want to know in the community.*

This list should be comprised of people you admire, have heard of, may have met, but none of whom you know well. These are people to whom you need an introduction and are hopeful of finding acquaintances who can forge those meetings. Social media sites like LinkedIn can be powerful tools to help accomplish this task.

[35]

c. *Companies that I admire and want to get to know.*

Start by writing a description of your ideal company, identifying the characteristics that you admire, then finding out which companies possess those or some of those qualities. As you create this list, depending on your mission, make modifications based on who you are meeting with, what information they may be able to share, etc. In other words, know your audience and be prepared to alter your list depending on what you learn about the companies you have already documented and others that may come to the forefront over time.

d. *Non-negotiables*.

The is a list of the top 20 items most important to you in your career search, or to generate more sales, or as you look for ways to get involved in your community, etc. Think of it as a value set of sorts. By way of example, some of the attributes on my top 20 list included: i) Kansas City-based, ii) entrepreneurial culture, open to new concepts/ideas, innovation, iii) embracing of technology, iv) management responsibility (i.e. manage and mentor a team), v) "work-life balance" (i.e. family-friendly environment with some scheduling flexibility), vi) opportunities for continued advancement, etc. Surely, your list will be different than mine, but I encourage you to be honest with yourself, be clear with your intentions, and consider things like geography, culture, technology, function, personal aspirations, compensation and benefit requirements, etc. when documenting your list.

3. **Begin to schedule networking meetings** — start with one, then build.

4. **Ask everyone you meet for the names of others you should meet**.

5. **Follow up**:
   a. Write a (hand-written) thank you note;
   b. Reach out to referrals;
   c. Complete other tasks discussed — it is critical that you keep your promises!

6. **Keep an open mind** — there are many pathways to success.

7. **Attend events**—become recognized and recognizable.

8. **Remember: You are always interviewing/selling/being watched!** Be the same person you want to be known as whether you are at home, at work, or in the community.

9. **Work toward achieving your goal(s)** (e.g. landing a job, building your sales pipeline, finding a new client, serving on a not-for-profit board, etc.).

10. **Keep networking!** Help others to network, too. Now that you have achieved your goal, identify your next goal, and actively pursue it. Remember that networking is FOR LIFE.

I hope you will come to agree that networking is both fun and important. Here is a real-life anecdote that may help bring the experience to life. It is a story a friend of mine, Danny Freeman, shared about his best networking experience:

[37]

> *In my experience, the most powerful possible result of networking is typically a job offer. Leading up to the summer of 2011, I was wrapping up an internship with a trading firm in Chicago and attempting to continue my experience in finance toward private equity ("PE") instead. For the folks who don't know the PE world, it is nearly impossible to achieve a job with a PE fund while in or having just completed college. I already had a couple of other internships under my belt in investment banking, so I certainly had a leg up, but finding a firm that would even give me the time of day was a huge challenge. I maximized my entire network, speaking with everyone in the industry who would take my call, and heavily leveraging my alumni network in Chicago, which was strong.*

Ultimately, I made several connections with whom I kept in touch, but needed to broaden my search if I had a prayer of landing a coveted private equity summer internship. The partner of one of the startup companies I was working for (a pharmacy benefit management auditing company) that had been previously owned by a private equity group, knew that the partner from that firm had started up a new shop of his own in Kansas City. She introduced me, and we hit it off right away via phone. I ended up flying down to KC on my own dime to show I was motivated and to get in front of the two partners. I nailed the offer as well as the internship, and ended up having a great summer with the group.

What do you love? What do you love to do? What gets you up and out of bed in the morning (besides your internal boss and the schedule you've now set for yourself) and excited to start your day? Where are you and what are you doing when you feel compelled to pinch yourself just to make sure it's real because you simply cannot believe that you get the opportunity to do it? Are you getting paid to engage in this awesome thing you love so much? Are you with people who propel you forward, who inspire you, who encourage and support you to do your very best? Who are they?

I feel passionately about my family and am particularly smitten with my son, whose wit, intelligence, kindness, compassion, and overall awesomeness I marvel at. Not unlike his dad, by the way! When I talk about my son to others, my voice changes. I feel differently. I smile… it's the condition I believe most mothers (all parents, really) have for their children.

I am passionate about the work that I am doing. Through the research of the Kauffman Foundation, I have learned and come to truly believe that entrepreneurship is the fuel for a stronger global economy, and a strong global economy benefits everyone. Engaging in dialogue with and about entrepreneurs is thrilling to me. I am energized by their passion, and our exchanges feed off one another.

I speak passionately about networking and its importance, because with every fiber of my being, I am convinced that the way that work, that life, that everything gets done is through relationships and relationship building—achieved primarily through networking.

Pascal Finette
entrepreneur
Mozilla

"As an entrepreneur, you are in the business of relationship building. You should see every interaction with someone who might be helpful to you and your business as a golden opportunity. Not making use of this opportunity in the best possible way is not only wasteful, but it might be the make-or-break moment of your company."

[39]

Use networking to advance your passions. When you go for coffee or lunch (or coffee, again) engage completely in the ensuing dialogue. Be fully present. Share a little piece of yourself. Your counterpart will respond in turn. You will each feed off of the other's enthusiasm. You will leave inspired. The rest of your day will be fueled by that inspiration.

And now that you are passionately prepared, it's time to move on into the mix—to hit the street!

[2.b] Make Your Four Lists:
List 1: People I Know

Whether you are networking as part of a career transition, to build a sales pipeline or to get more ingrained in the community, it is important to communicate with people you know — especially in order to get to know others who you don't. Get started on your networking journey by making a preliminary list of people you know — whom you plan to contact — to discuss your goals and aspirations. The list can be as long or as short as necessary. Try to begin with at least five good contacts, that is, people who you are certain will take an initial meeting with you; you can always come back later to add to your list.

Not sure whose names to write down? Start with people you have worked with in the community on volunteer projects, friends you have interacted with socially whom you admire for their professional activities, folks you know from your congregation, the parents of your children's schoolmates and soccer team, etc. So, let's start there:

Name	How I Know Him/Her	Phone Number(s)	Email Address	Notes
1.				
2.				
3.				
4.				
5.				

EXERCISE

[2. c] Make Your Four Lists:
List 2: People I Want to Know

As you begin networking — and throughout your networking lifetime — there will always be people you want to get to know — in your community and beyond. To begin to breach the divide between the people you know and the people you would like to get to know, make a list comprised of names of those you admire, have heard of, may even have met but don't know well but would like to. You will need introductions to these individuals and, to do so, will need to puzzle together a web of connections that will enable you to forge relationships with would be contacts. Once you have a list, you can start to connect dots — by asking the folks from "List 1: People I know," [41] connections via LinkedIn, etc. We'll get to that soon…

Name	Company	Why I want to know him/her	People I know who may know this person	Notes
1.				
2.				
3.				
4.				
5.				
6.				
7.				
8.				
9.				
10.				
11.				
12.				
13.				
14.				
15.				
16.				
17.				
18.				
19.				
20.				

EXERCISE

[2.d] Make Your Four Lists:
List 3: Companies of Interest

Whatever your motivation for networking, as you consider your approach, there will be companies you admire and want to get to know. Begin by writing a description of your ideal company, identifying the characteristics that you admire, then finding out which companies possess those or some of those qualities. As you create this list for yourself, depending on your mission, you will need to make modifications based on who you meet with, what information they may be able to share, etc. In other words, know your audience and be prepared to be flexible depending on what you learn about the companies you have already documented and others that may come to the forefront.

Industries of Interest: EX: Healthcare

1.
2.
3.
4.
5.

Qualities of an Ideal Company: EX: Independent hospital

1.
2.
3.
4.
5.

Description of My Ideal Company:
EX: I am interested in small, privately-held, independent hospitals
that provide outpatient services to the local community and
are looking to grow and expand their service offerings.

EXERCISE

[2.e] Make Your Four Lists:
List 4: Non-Negotiables

Start thinking about what it is that you are looking for. What do you care about? Consider the question, "What are the top 20 items most important to me in my [career search]?" Not in career transition? Replace the words, "…important to me in my career search," with something like, "…important to me in order to generate more sales," or "…important to me as I look for ways to get involved in my community." The point is, understand the type of person or organization that will be meaningful — in a big or small way — as you embark on your networking quest.

Be honest with yourself. Be clear of your intentions. Consider [43] things like geography, culture, technology, function, personal aspirations.

Sample attributes:

1. Kansas City-based

2. Entrepreneurial culture, open to new concepts/ ideas, innovation

3. Embracing of technology

4. Management responsibility (i.e. manage and mentor a team)

5. "Work-Life Balance" (i.e. family-friendly environment with some scheduling flexibility)

6. Opportunities for continued advancement

7. A sense of ownership (i.e. profit and loss responsibility, key deliverables that drive company success)

8. Company with a sense of corporate social responsibility that encourages community involvement

9. Insight into multiple parts of the business, industry

10. Minimum salary requirements

Your turn. Create your Top 20 List of Non-Negotiables.

1.	11.
2.	12.
3.	13.
4.	14.
5.	15.
6.	16.
7.	17.
8.	18.
9.	19.
10.	20.

EXERCISE

[2.f] LinkedIn Profile

As you prepare to create or update your LinkedIn profile, allow me to share a funny story about how I first began using LinkedIn. One of my early networking meetings was with a recruiter named Melissa Watkins from OMNI Employment. Though I was not connecting with Melissa to engage her recruiting services, we were eager to meet one another in a networking capacity. During our initial get together, Melissa gave me one of the best pieces of networking advice I received as I was getting started.

We met one morning for coffee at Panera Bread, one of my favorite spots for coffee (or lunch). Melissa asked me a lot of questions about how I was conducting my search, who I was talking with, etc. That's when she said: "I assume your LinkedIn profile is 100% complete, right?" I laughed in response, as I wasn't even registered with LinkedIn at the time. She politely suggested I rectify this. She told me that of the last five or so positions for which she had conducted searches, she had filled three via connections at LinkedIn. I went directly home and completed my LinkedIn profile, which meant filling in my career history, educational background, interests, photo, etc. It also meant gathering referrals from people I'd worked with. I opted to include a variety of people—former teammates, direct reports, managers, customers, peer volunteers, etc. Nervous as I was to ask for those referrals, I was grateful and humbled when everyone I asked to write a few sentences on my behalf readily complied. In many cases, they also requested that I return the favor, which I was delighted to do.

I quickly went from about five connections to hundreds. Today, I have more than 1,000. Note, however, that it is not the quantity or volume of contacts that matters—in fact, I do not accept all invitations that I receive. Those that I do accept are based on the potential quality of those connections — that's what's important. When you ask to link to someone, or when someone asks to link to you, it is important to have a good sense for why he or she is a valuable connection. >>>

EXERCISE

[2.f] LinkedIn Profile [continued]

And by the way, when you ask someone to connect, be sure to write them a personal message—do not take the lazy way out by using the standard LinkedIn language. When people fail to tell me who they are, how we met and/or why we should connect, I, more often than not, ignore the request to connect. Another important aside: For each new qualified connection that you make, you loosely connect to their entire database of connections. Soon, you will have general access to millions—yes millions— of additional people. For example, with my 1,000+ contacts (a number that is continuously growing), I have access to about 8.8 million professionals. In this case, quantity IS important, and here's why: You can utilize LinkedIn to conduct informal focus groups and quickly gather information that could take you much longer if you went about it on your own. Allow me to illustrate.

[45]

When I was consulting locally to McCownGordon Construction, the project they asked me to take on had to do with an industry and function that I knew NOTHING about. I entered a question into LinkedIn—I asked, "Is anyone using a good CMMS program?" If you think that I knew at the time what a CMMS program was, you are mistaken. However, I did know that anyone who bothered to answer my question would know. Thankfully, I was right! Two people, who I did not (and still do not) know, responded with awesome answers. One of them—Kevin—even sent me a 150-page research report on the best such systems, a report I would not otherwise have had access to. That's the power of LinkedIn (and of networking).

LinkedIn is also great for job seekers and salespeople who are trying to learn more about companies of interest. Through the site's advanced search feature, you can enter a company name and discover people in your network—or your network's network—who have connections to that company. Through your network, you can also request introductions to others you'd like to meet. Very powerful. >>>

EXERCISE

[2.f] LinkedIn Profile [continued]

Pascal Finette
entrepreneur
Mozilla

"When networking through LinkedIn, never, and I mean never, send out an invite using the standard invite text. The signal you are sending me by doing this is: You are not worth the time for me to change this text and I just want to connect with you to add you to my collection. Instead, write a short, personal message which sells the other person on the idea to connect to you. This is best achieved by making a small ask. Say something like, 'I would love to stay in touch with you and ask you every once in a while for your advice on XYZ.'"

Obviously, though I have focused on LinkedIn, there are other social media sites that are invaluable, such as Facebook, Twitter, and others. That said, if you are going to pick or only have time to devote energy to one site, for business networking, I believe LinkedIn is the best at the time of this writing.

So, let's get back to creating your profile. By now, you know that LinkedIn is an extremely useful means of building out your network. By completing your profile and beginning to build your connections with people you know well, you will be able to connect to hundreds, thousands, even millions of people. It is easiest to document and save your LinkedIn profile on your own computer using a software program like Microsoft Word. Once you are satisfied with it, you can cut and paste your profile into LinkedIn and you'll be good to go! >>>

EXERCISE

[2.f] LinkedIn Profile [continued]

Here are the sections that you should work on:

Section	Description	About Me
Headline	Provide your profile viewers with a way to understand and remember who you are with a brief, memorable description. Think of the headline as the slogan for the brand of you, such as "Experienced Executive" or "Marketing Professional with 25 years experience." For inspiration, take a look at the LinkedIn profiles of others who you admire and respect.	
Summary	Develop a summary statement that is akin to a résumé overview or the way you might describe yourself in a well-written cover letter. Be concise and confident as you describe your goals and qualifications in a few paragraphs or bullet points.	
Specialties Experience Volunteer Experience Skills & Experience Interests	In these sections, it is important for you to use keywords and phrases that a potential networking contact, recruiter or hiring manager might type into a search engine to find people like you. Good examples of such keywords can be found in the LinkedIn profiles of others who you resemble or would like to resemble, of job descriptions of positions that you are interested in pursuing.	
Education	Highlight your complete education. Include areas of study and degrees from all institutions you've attended. Include your majors and minors, if you have one, honors and awards you received, as well highlights of the organizations/clubs that you were involved in. You should also include information about study abroad and summer programs. A few additional items of note: ■ **Experience**: For each of your positions, include title, company, dates, description of accomplishments for each of your positions ■ **Volunteer Experience**: For each volunteer activity, include organization, role(s), dates of involvement	

>>>

EXERCISE

[2.f] LinkedIn Profile [continued]

Here are the sections that you should work on, *continued*:

Section	Description	About Me
Recommendations	Seek to gain credibility through a series of diverse, third party endorsements. Aim for at least five recommendations. These are brief statements from people you have worked with (both employers and co-workers are appropriate), fellow volunteers, professors, clients, mentors, et al. LinkedIn makes it easy for you to request recommendations and review each one as they are completed, prior to posting them on your profile.	
Public Profile URL	Customize your public profile URL address (i.e. change it from a random series of letters and numbers to your name or something that is similarly descriptive). Your newly customized URL should look something like: **linkedin.com/in/yourname**. This URL is useful for business cards, email signatures, résumés and the like.	
Photograph	Add a professional, high quality photo of yourself to your profile.	

Remember that LinkedIn is a living, breathing, ever changing thing. Go back often to check for updates, be sure to provide your status or thoughts on a relatively frequent basis (e.g. at least once per week) so that your profile rises to the top in relevant search results. Also, consider adding a link to your personal blog or website (can also be your company's website or that of a not-for-profit board on which you sit), include articles that you have written, join appropriate groups, etc. There are many ways to bolster your profile and to leverage the power of LinkedIn as a means of building your professional network. You can add all of this information, join groups, incorporate applications, etc. by going to LinkedIn > Profile > Edit Profile. Oh... but the very first step, if you haven't done so already, is to go to **linkedin.com** to register.

THREE

CHANGING IT UP

After a couple of immersive chapters on getting into the networking rhythm, I hope you have begun to formulate a list of people you know, or want to get to know. So bring out that list and start making contact.

Set a daily goal for yourself—how many people you will get in touch with every day, how many appointments per week you will try for, and once you start meeting with the people you know, begin asking them to connect you to the people you hope to get to know — AND for the names of other people THEY suggest will be helpful. Then it's simply a question of getting those meetings scheduled.

For me, asking for the meeting has always been easiest and most effective by email. For the sake of efficiency and consistency, I recommend that you create an email template that provides a brief introduction, explains what you are looking for, and suggests a date and time to meet. Here is the template that I used when I first started networking. Most of the specific content is no longer relevant for me, but interestingly, I think that every request I have made since has been some variation of this format:

TO: Max Speakman

SUBJECT: Introduction from Charlene Smith

Hello, Max,

Charlene Smith referred me to you; my name is Alana Muller. I would love an opportunity to visit with you, in a networking capacity, over coffee or lunch to learn more about what you are doing professionally and your career path.

By way of background, I have been an executive at Sprint for the past 10 years and made the career decision to leave the company this past June. While there, I was granted a number of terrific general management experiences, serving in a variety of capacities, most notably in the wireless data marketing area with responsibility for managing the music portfolio and merchandising the company's wireless data services overall. Prior to that, I spent time as a director in the talent management group with responsibility for executive and leadership development, performance management and succession planning for the organization's 60,000 employees.

Now, I am seeking opportunities at mid-market companies here in the Kansas City area that are looking for leadership to help them to achieve growth.

Please let me know your willingness and availability to meet over the next few weeks. I will also follow up with a phone call. Your consideration is appreciated.

Best regards,

Alana

Alana Muller
123.456.7890
Alana@coffeelunchcoffee.com

Your message, of course, will be different from mine, but just keep in mind that what you want to do is tell a story—your story, and to lead with a subject line that will compel your new contact to open the email, e.g. "introduction from so and so." You will have a chance to build your own email introduction at the end of this chapter.

Incidentally, if you decide to call rather than write, whether you reach the person live or via voicemail, start with something like: "Hello, Max. My name is Alana Muller. I received your contact information from Charlene Smith." This will help you establish credibility and provide an immediate frame of reference for your target.

DO NOT send your résumé with your meeting request. You must, simply must, resist the urge to do so. I know that this is not relevant for those of you not now seeking new job opportunities, but to those for whom it is relevant, if you feel compelled to eventually send your contact a résumé prior to your meeting, don't send it until the day before your meeting, with an email confirming the details of your meeting.

Earlier in this chapter I mentioned that what you want to do when reaching out to a new or previously known contact is to tell a story. In fact, storytelling is an important tool in the master networker's arsenal, and a skill we should all embrace, hone, and become proficient at. Stories draw us in, they paint a picture. They make the listener feel as if they are right there in the story with the storyteller.

Seven Story Learning, a company founded by my friend, Andrew Nemiccolo, helps companies develop their natural story-sharing abilities in order to influence, lead, and sell more effectively. Andrew says that more than ever before, stories remain one of the most potent ways to deeply connect with others, a belief I share.

Andrew Nemiccolo
offers this stellar networking advice:

Listening is more important than telling. Telling other people your story increases your chances of being remembered. Listening to their stories increases your chances of being liked! Networking is equal parts storytelling and "story-listening" (i.e., deeply active and generous listening that helps someone else to share their story).

For your own storytelling purposes, I suggest you develop a repertoire, or toolkit, of stories for different situations. Having a variety of stories ready in your "StoryBank" enables you to adapt your communication to suit the party with which you are engaged in dialogue. And, remember, good stories have always been about people overcoming conflict and growing in the process. There are more complex structures, but in the end, this is the essence of understanding the core of stories. In fact, stories of lessons learned from failure are some of the most powerful stories we can share — they are a sign of strength, not weakness.

Another colleague, Craig Wortmann, an entrepreneur, author, and professor at the University of Chicago Booth School of Business (my alma mater!), is also someone I consider a master storyteller. His book, *What's Your Story: Using Stories to Ignite Performance and Be More Successful*, illustrates how stories can help to address common performance challenges around leadership, strategic selling, and motivation. It offers valuable lessons for anyone in business.

Effective storytelling can help us become better networkers. The way we tell our story can help set us apart, ensure that we are memorable (in a good way) to our new contacts, even after the meeting is over.

Prepare for networking encounters by thinking ahead to a few great stories you can tell to get your message across, stories that bring to life what you do best, and how you've done it effectively in the past.

If you are not good at telling stories off the cuff, go the extra step and write them down in advance. **What was the situation? Who was there? Where did it take place? What was the big moment, or punch line, and what does the story illustrate about you? If you've written down the story, reread it and cut out any extraneous detail, anything that creates distracting noise around the main point.**

Then practice—in front of the mirror if that's helpful, or with a friend, or even in front of your dog, if she is your favorite audience. If you have what I refer to as a "networking buddy," someone you know you can count on to give you honest, constructive feedback on your networking efforts, read it to them.

As you listen to your own story, think of the last time you heard a really well-told story. "As the autumn sun shone on the maple tree with its burnt orange and red leaves, was the air crisp and could you taste fall in the air? Could you smell the aroma of the pumpkin bread, the nutmeg and cinnamon bursting forth as the silver tin with the budding loaf peeking out over its edge was pulled from the oven?" Yum. You get the picture...

Are you a fan of the television show "Mad Men?" Right after the main character, Don Draper, and his partners leave their corporate parent to go out on their own, Don, who is considered the most creative advertising man on Madison Avenue, sits down with *Advertising Age* magazine to do an interview. But it's clear that he's not seeing the interview as an opportunity to tell his story in a compelling way, and thus help promote his new agency. It's obvious to the reporter (and to the viewer) that Don just wants to get the interview over with. He does not engage with the interviewer, and the resulting article is a dud that does nothing to put the new ad agency in a new light, and in fact has the opposite of the intended effect: it makes Don seem arrogant and uninteresting. When his colleagues point out that he's missed a chance to make them all look good, at first he is annoyed. He is a great creative director, so why does he also have to be responsible for giving great interview? That's not in his job description. But after dwelling on it a bit more, Don decides maybe his colleagues are right. He acts to correct the mistake by taking another newspaper up on their offer to interview him. When he sits down with the reporter this time around, he owns it. He relishes telling the story of how and why he and his partners decided to go it on their own, and he also acknowledges his own accomplishments. He always knew the value of storytelling when it came to telling the story of a product, for the purposes of creating a great ad, but he's now discovered that it's also an important tool in connecting with other people. We don't know for sure, but our guess is that the resulting article profiling Don Draper put the agency over the top.

For those of you who are using networking as part of an effort to find employment, the time you spend developing a story will serve you well when you are sitting in an interview. A core technique to use in preparing for an interview is to (a) realize that you will be asked questions that begin with phrases like, "Tell me about a time when you...," "Describe

a situation in which you...," and (b) prepare and practice several stories you can use in a variety of situations when those questions are asked.

Once you've gotten your story down, get ready for that first set of meetings. Here are a few helpful hints I always keep in the back of my mind:

1. **Be Fearless.**

2. **Start with people you know—branch out to those they know**.

3. **Ask for introductions**—cold is okay, warm is better, hot is best, in other words:

   - *Cold*: You contact someone out of the blue whom you have never met without the ability to say that you were "referred by so-and-so." Chances of getting that contact to take a meeting with you are relatively low.

   - *Warm*: You reach out to the contact, say that you were referred by so-and-so and ask for a meeting. If the contact knows and respects so-and-so, you will probably get a meeting.

- ***Hot***: So-and-so sends a note to the networking prospect with a brief introduction and encourages the two of you to get together. In this case, a meeting is highly likely assuming so-and-so is respected by the prospect.

Almost ten years ago, I recall that my incredibly well-connected friend Scott Slabotsky urged me to meet his colleague Tim Hannan, who was doing work similar to mine back in the day. For whatever reason, I didn't follow up until Scott reminded me of this potential connect four years later, when I set out on my own. It still took me a few months, but I finally did reach out to Tim, sending a note that looks very similar to the template I shared with you earlier in this chapter. Tim and I exchanged a few emails and finally agreed to meet at Starbucks; it was a meeting that changed everything for me.

[55]

Tim and I met at 8:30 a.m. because he needed to get back to the office for a 9:30 a.m. meeting. Since we had only thirty minutes to spend, we got right down to business.

Tim shared a bit about his background, and I told him about mine. He asked me several very pointed questions about my interests and aspirations, and I answered. Then he began rattling off names of people I should connect with, and when I say "rattling off," I mean listing people faster than I could write them down. But in any case he told me not to bother taking notes, he would follow up quickly with their names and contact details. He wasn't kidding.

By the time I got back to my house about thirty minutes later, I had an email from Tim waiting for me, which said: "It was a pleasure to meet with you this morning and learn more about what type of opportunities you are interested in pursuing. Attached are some of the contacts we discussed. Please call me at your convenience and I can give you more info. Good luck." Attached were eight digital business cards.

I'm no fool. I picked up the phone right away and called Tim, who took the call and proceeded to share tidbits about each contact with me — information that was not on their business cards. He told me specifically why he thought each of them might make a worthwhile connection for me. Armed with information and focusing on why I was trying to contact each specific person, I started reaching out immediately.

Of the eight, six quickly responded to me and agreed to meet. Here's what I got from those six — I hope that you will glean from each of these brief stories lessons that may be relevant to your own networking quests.

1. **Pat**: a venture capitalist doing deals all over the country, Pat and I had a fruitful email exchange. He asked me for my résumé which he shared with some of his contacts. He also asked me an awesome question that I think everyone should ask themselves, especially when they are transitioning in their careers. "What would you love to do and in what capacity?"

2. **Mike**: Another VC guy, with whom it turns out I have several other contacts in common. We hit it off right away. His areas of expertise are life sciences and animal health. He told me about companies in the Kansas City area that were growing and potentially in need of leadership.

3. **Melanie**: A financial expert, a CFO type. We met for lunch and became immediate, fast friends. Over the next year or so, we crossed paths many more times and were able to share mutually useful information with one another.

4. **Marshall**: A property developer who graciously took me to lunch. A long-time Kansas City resident, we spent time sharing our individual histories and telling one another about our families. His kindly nature, advocacy, and generous advice gave me inspiration and encouragement. As I went on to start my own consulting company, he became an important resource to me and served as a subject matter expert on topics related to commercial real estate that I would not otherwise have had ready access to.

5. **Pam**: Pam is a successful banking executive and entrepreneur. Over breakfast one morning at the Classic Cup, Pam and I had one of the most candid, most useful conversations that I had during my career transition. She patiently listened to my story, asked insightful questions about my interests, and gave thoughtful, relevant input on the pros and cons to my plan — not to discourage me, but to provide me with a reality/sanity check so that I would go into my next gig with eyes wide open. She remains an important and trusted friend.

6. **Teresa**: Ah, and then there was Teresa. I remember that date and time perfectly. I met Teresa for coffee at a little café near her office. It was Halloween morning. We briefly shared intros, talked about our kids' intended Halloween costumes, and began to exchange information. She told me that she was a rep for a major commercial insurance firm and that her client base consisted mainly of construction firms. She wondered who I wanted to meet in that industry. I told her that I knew next to nothing about construction, but that I had heard about one firm where the culture matched my values, and I wanted to meet someone there. She said: "Perfect. I'm taking the CFO to the Chiefs game on Sunday. I'll ask him if there's anything going on there for which you would be a fit." Not knowing whether I would hear from her again, imagine my delight when on Sunday night Teresa emailed me to say that the CFO would be expecting my call! Turns out the CFO, Jeff, is my friend Angie's husband — Angie is a former colleague from Sprint who even hosted my baby shower, and though we hadn't been in touch in some time, the couple were still on my holiday card list. I called Jeff, and, to make a long story short, six weeks later I had landed a major eight-month consulting assignment with his company, one that would lead to my current assignment, in other words, A SERIOUS GAME CHANGER.

So what are the lessons I learned that are relevant to your own networking?

- Ask for the meeting.
- At the meeting, ask for referrals to other potential contacts.
- Don't wait. Reach out to those potential contacts—ask for the meeting. I could have been learning from and networking with others a lot more quickly if I had acted on Scott's first urging to meet Tim.
- You never know where the meeting might take you, immediately or down the road.
- Tell stories.
- Don't despair if you don't hear back right away. People get busy and their lack of response is not a reflection on you. With patience and follow up, chances are good that you will eventually get time with your contacts — even if it takes a bit of extra time and effort.

Same Time Next Week

My friend, Kristin Schultz, has a unique approach to networking which I love. She gets together with the same individual — a peer — every week. Their range of topics varies, but like a devoted Rotarian or Chamber of Commerce board member, the two are committed to their weekly gathering and use one another as a sounding board, voice of reason, personal coach and mentor. Here's how Kristin describes their meetings: *Every Thursday morning over the past year, I've made a point of having coffee with my friend, Amy. It began because our paths weren't crossing naturally; but quickly established itself as a regular meeting with professional, personal and philanthropic implications. Our conversations range from elements of good design and education policy to facing the issues of aging parents; and lately, some interesting strategies for a new business endeavor. Because we both actively look for interesting groups and activities, we cross-pollinate one another's network and inhabit our own kooky Venn diagram of people, knowledge and experiences. It hasn't taken much discipline to preserve that time on my schedule; its value having expanded into real friendship, family connection and the unexpected benefits of no particular agenda.*

EXERCISE

[3.a] Email Introduction

Your turn to build an email introduction for yourself. Use the following matrix to create something catchy, meaningful and succinct to grab your targets' attention:

Action Step	Description	Your Response
Subject Line of the Email	Say something to encourage the recipient to open your message such as who you were referred by.	
Introductory Paragraph	Set up the message. Tell your recipient: ■ Who referred you? By stating this up front, your new contact is more likely to read your message and respond so that he/she does not let down your mutual acquaintance. ■ What is your name? ■ What do you want from him/her?	
Brief Background	Share a few sentences about your professional background, experience, company, etc.	
Aspirational Statement	Tell the recipient a little about your goals. It will help him/her to get a glimpse of how he/she may be of assistance to you.	
Ask for the Sale	Request a meeting. Suggest a day or time to meet and/or ask about his/her availability.	
Close	Thank your reader for his/her consideration, offer a valediction (e.g. "Yours truly," "Sincerely," or "Best regards") and provide your full name, phone number and email address.	

>>>

EXERCISE

[3.a] Email Introduction [continued]

Now, put it all together so that you can cut and paste it into an email:

Subject Line: _____

Dear [CONTACT'S NAME],

Best Regards,

[YOUR FIRST NAME]

[YOUR FIRST AND LAST NAME]
[YOUR PHONE NUMBER(S)]
[YOUR EMAIL ADDRESS]
[OPTIONAL: LINKEDIN PROFILE URL, TWITTER HANDLE and/or WEBSITE]

EXERCISE

[3.b] Phone Introduction

Similar to the email introduction is the phone introduction. If you decide to call rather than write, whether to reach the person live or need to leave a message, start with something like, *"Hello, Max. My name is Alana Muller. I received your contact information from Charlene Smith…"* Yes, just like the email template. It will help you to establish credibility and provide a frame of reference for your target.

Borrowing from the language of your email introduction, write your phone or voice message introduction in the lines that follow.

[81]

EXERCISE

[3.c] What's Your Story?

Beyond an "elevator pitch" or 30-second commercial, you will need an arsenal of stories that will serve to engage your contacts, share a little bit of yourself and illustrate your history, background, experience and expertise. Seven Story Learning offers the following "CHAPTER" framework for building your stories. No doubt, you have many chapters in the story of your life — why not give it a shot! Try documenting a story or two of your own.

Seven Story Learning CHAPTER Story Building Model

Your Story

C	Conflict	Lack of Conflict is Boring!	
		Clarify the conflict – not just the business or technical issue, but the larger human issue.	
		Goldilocks conflicts are "just right" for the story.	
H	Hero	Who overcame the conflict?	
		Introduce any allies and mentors who helped the hero.	
A	Anticipation	Why is it important to overcome the conflict?	
		Narrate the internal and external struggle.	
		Emotion and uncertainty build tension and curiosity.	
P	Peak	This how you solved the conflict.	
		What exactly did YOU do?	
		Describe it in human terms, not technical jargon.	
T	Transformation	Clarify how you're different now as a result of overcoming the conflict.	
		What did you learn?	
		Does it inspire you (and others) to further action?	
E	Explain	Demonstrate how you're STILL different now.	
		Important for the "What's Your Weakness?" question.	
R	Relate	Is the story relevant to your listener?	
		Have you shared a story in a way that will make others want to share *their* story with you?	

[FOUR]

TIME TO TAKE THE PLUNGE

It's not easy to go out into the world and connect with strangers, hoping to impress them, be of use to them, get a piece of information from them that could become a game changer for you, perhaps even make a new friend. That's especially true if you are somewhat introverted.

In the bestselling book *Quiet: The Power of Introverts in a World That Can't Stop Talking*, author Susan Cain makes a good case for how prevalent and underrated introverts are in our alpha world, but it's still tough for some people to break out of their comfort zones, to place calls or send emails to new contacts, whether "cold," "warm" or "hot," or to enter a room filled with bustling, confident networkers at a meet-up or other event. As I've reiterated a few times already in the course of this book, I love networking, and yet, some aspects of it do not come naturally even to me.

So how do we take the plunge, with grace, acumen, wit, and purpose? And by the way, how do we do it while being self-confident and at the same time humble? Isn't that an oxymoron?

Heather Kostelnick
Project and Process Management Professional

"How do I connect with others? I make eye contact.
I talk first. I ask them something about what they are
buying, or wearing, or doing. I set up lunches and
meetings. I make connections because it is the right
thing to do, because I am curious, and because we need
each other to start and to finish our work. And, it's fun!
And, finding out that I have something to offer through
it all is a great bonus and keeps me going."

I recently listened to a National Public Radio story broadcast on "All Things Considered." The host, Renee Montagne, was talking with Lawrence Weschler, a *New Yorker* writer who covered Poland in the 1980's and 90's, and who was now commenting on the recent death of Polish poetess Wislawa Szymborska, a Nobel Laureate for Literature.

I must admit, I had not previously heard of Ms. Szymborska. That said, when I listened to excerpts from her work, I wished that I had. But my main point is not about her poetry; instead, it's about how Mr. Weschler described her. He said: "**(Szymborska) was deeply profound but she carried her gravity lightly. She was extremely clear. She was very, very modest.**" Lovely, I thought, to be perceived as "deeply profound," yet with the ability to manage the weight of it so effortlessly — to be able to share information with others in a way that doesn't bash them over the head with a sledgehammer, but rather, provides them with useful, meaningful data, in a clear and inviting way. What a wonderful characteristic to possess.

And then I thought about how that might apply to our topic, and it occurred to me that we are each endless wells of information and experience. Few of us have earned Nobel Prizes in Literature (or in Networking), but there are areas of expertise we have mastered.

The trick is to be able to quickly parse through and assess our personal databanks in order to come up with the right detail, story or response at the right time, and to convey that information to others in a way that is understandable and actionable. When we do engage with our contacts, we must meet them where they are, invite them into our worlds, share information with them openly and in an inviting manner, in a way that authentically represents who we are, and offers the best chance of truly connecting. And, perhaps beginning a relationship.

On what topics are you "deeply profound?" Are you an expert or do you have a strong, thoughtful opinion on a particular issue, and can you present that point of view in a way that is clear and can be embraced by others? What data can you share that will serve a valuable and meaningful purpose to your contacts? And, finally, are you prepared to listen first, and then to articulate in the context of the challenges your contacts face? If so, you will establish trust and come to be known as a credible source of information, a valuable resource for others.

Oh, and as for the part about how Ms. Szymborska "carried her gravity lightly," Mr. Weschler may only have meant that she didn't take herself too seriously, but I like to think he was also observing that she had a sense of humor, that she made others laugh. And there IS a place for humor in business, and in networking. Smiles and laughter are, after all, contagious, and most of us have a better time, and, I would argue, are more productive, when a little levity is part of the mix. So even when interacting with people in a professional capacity, lead with a smile, share a laugh or two. It's been scientifically proven that there are actual health benefits associated with laughter…

Now that you are armed with poetry and a laugh, here are some concrete suggestions to keep in mind as you take the plunge:

1. **ATTITUDE**: Make a decision to believe that you are a great networker. Expect to have fun. Though the idea can be daunting, the rewards of networking will pay dividends for

years to come. By reaching out to and helping others, by always saying "YES!," you will build a solid professional network. And stay true to the advice of Denise Upah Mills, master connector and entrepreneur: "Networking is just friends helping friends."

2. **PROCESS**: Determine an approach that will work for you. My tried and true approach is coffee-lunch-coffee. Yours may involve a morning of email outreach followed by two afternoon meetings, and a social networking event that evening. But whatever your process, be sure to set specific goals, chronicle everything in a written or online journal, and follow up quickly. In setting goals, consider how many new people you will seek to develop relationships with each day, each week, each month, each year. Enlist a "buddy" to hold you accountable. My original goal when setting out on my own was to "touch," via email, phone call or face-to-face meeting, fifteen people per week. Now that I have full time work commitments, my goal is closer to five to ten people per week. Come up with your number and relentlessly pursue that goal.

3. **PREPARE**: Create your lists. Include people you know in the community, people you want to know, companies you admire and want to get to know, and the top 20 items that are most important to you in terms of whatever quest you are on, i.e., whether job search, fact-finding mission, or continuing education and stimulation. And don't forget to do your homework.

4. **KNOW YOUR STORY**: Be prepared with your key stories, those that describe who you are, what you do, what you believe in, how you operate. Take time in advance to craft an introductory email, telling them you would like a few minutes of their time to meet in a networking capacity to get to know them and learn more about their professional journey. Also, prepare your personal introduction. You may have heard the expression "30-second commercial" or "elevator pitch." Now is the time

to implement that concept. Be prepared to say who you are, what you do, what your aspirations are, or any other pertinent information that will help your new contact connect with you. It also helps to have a business card with all your relevant contact info, which may sound old-fashioned, but it's still effective.

I've advised you to clarify your goals, to be prepared, to have fun with it—all essential components as you begin to hit the streets, and embark on your networking adventure. But there is another thing that you should consider, as you are about to take the plunge, and that is "What sort of first impression do I make?" By that I don't necessarily mean how well-dressed you are, or what your hairstyle signals, but rather, are you doing all the basic things your mother told you way back when, such as standing up straight, looking your contact in the eye, shaking their hand firmly, etc.? I know this seems like basic stuff, and it is, but even pros can forget, when it comes to what makes for a great first impression.

A few tips on what makes for a great first impression:

- **Exude energy**. People love to be around others who radiate energy, optimism and enthusiasm. By so doing, you will appear self-confident, happy and fun to be with. Be sure to smile — the twinkle in your eye will draw 'em in.

- **Offer a firm handshake and make eye contact**. I've been teased for years for the quality of my handshake… can't help it! As a child, my parents told us how impressed our grandfather would be if we greeted him with a firm handshake — the advice stuck! Don't break your contact's hand, but show 'em you mean business by looking them in the eye (more on this in a moment), putting your hand out in greeting, smiling and saying hello. You will display great self-confidence by doing so.

- **Be authentic. Be human**. Show a genuine interest in your contact. Establish rapport. Ask questions and listen actively. Your truthfulness, honesty, authenticity will shine through.

- **Clearly convey your key message(s)**. We've already worked on your 30-second commercial/elevator pitch. Stay on point. Make sure you articulate the information you desire.
- **Relax**. Take a deep breath. You're doing great.

Truth told, we all have our unfortunate tendencies; I certainly have a few of my own…for example, my eyes are hazel and are predisposed to change colors. I used to think that had to do with the level of the light in the room or outside, but I have learned otherwise over the past few years. Turns out my eyes tend toward brown during periods of stress — the greater the stress level, the darker the color. Conversely, during periods of calm, my eyes blaze green. It is a phenomenon that I cannot directly control. Now that I have let out my secret, you will have a better sense of my state of mind next time we see one another.

Oh, and then there is this little gem: When I am caught off guard, surprised, embarrassed and sometimes when I'm mad, I blush. Ugh. It is so awful! It, too, is difficult to control. I wish that I could, and I try, but often to no avail. I realize that this is not that uncommon, but it is just one of those things that many of us contend with that I just despise!

Lest I reveal too much and share with you all of my unfortunate non-verbals, I will stop there. But, I ask you (rhetorically, of course), what are your non-verbals? That is, what does your body language say about how you are feeling, what you think of the person you are with, how good you feel about the conversation? Have you found a way to manage them? Can others read you like a book, even when you think your reactions are remaining under the surface?

So what is one to do? Here are a few ideas:

1. **EYE CONTACT**: Focus, focus, focus and practice. Do this until it becomes less of a chore and more of a habit. Consciously make the decision and the effort not to look away. The ancillary benefits here include a boost in self-confidence and more of a connection with the person you are interacting with.

2. **SWEATING AND LOSS OF BREATH**: Okay this one is difficult, and perhaps not to be discussed in polite company. But it happens. So here's what you do: Focus on your breathing. In through your mouth, out through your nose. Slow down your breathing. (Caution: don't hyperventilate!) But as your heart slows to a more regulated pace, you will begin to feel calmer, cooler, ready for the conversation. Oh, and if it's summer and you're in Kansas City in the 100 degree heat, meet inside, where it's air conditioned!

3. **KNOW WHAT YOUR HANDS ARE DOING**: Take a few days and pay attention to what you do with your hands during conversations. Are you animated? Do you throw your hands around wildly when you're talking? Are you a hand wringer? Be mindful of how you sit, and where you put your hands. Think about placing your hands in a position that does not distract from the discussion, perhaps neatly folded in front of you or on the table or, if you must gesture from time to time, keep it simple and relatively small.

[89]

It is true, in our American culture, that "rugged individualism" has long been what is revered. We think of Lewis and Clark, going off together to explore the West, or someone like Teddy Roosevelt, or Abraham Lincoln, people who are larger than life, whether in myth, or in reality. Individualism and integrity are still essential ingredients, of course, but in these new days, it is connectivity that rules. The internet and social media have fueled these connections, but cooperation and interaction are also increasingly necessary in every realm, so that we can survive, and so that we can thrive. I like to think of networking not as a means to an end, but as a way of being. Improving your networking skills really means becoming a human being who is better at connecting with others. There will always be lone rangers who are out there going it alone. But wouldn't you rather be someone with a lot of satisfying relationships, who helps and is helped by others?

Are you ready to take the plunge? Go on. Jump in!

EXERCISE

[4.a] 30-Second Commercial or Elevator Speech

Create a succinct description of who you are, your background, strengths and objectives. Include just enough to intrigue the other party — their continued interest and follow up questions will let you know whether you have done a good job of presenting yourself.

Here are some 30-second commercials to get you thinking about your own version:

Sample 1: *"I am seeking opportunities in the Kansas City area with small- to mid-market sized companies looking for leadership to help them achieve growth or enter new markets. I want to be part of a collaborative culture and a company at which I would have a seat at the leadership table — a place where I can contribute to the strategy and future of the organization and to have decision-making authority and accountability."*

Sample 2: *"My company, Kauffman FastTrac,® is a not-for-profit, educational organization that provides entry to the entrepreneurial ecosystem for current and aspiring business owners, before — during — and after the startup process. It does so by licensing a series of content to third party organizations around the world that deliver FastTrac® courses to entrepreneurs based on our proven methodology. We help entrepreneurs to start and grow successful companies."*

Remember: Whether you already have an elevator pitch or personal commercial, ask others for feedback to ensure that you are saying what you think you are saying. This is an evergreen process — you should constantly refine your pitch. It will always, always be a work in process and you will become clearer and more articulate about what you want, need, are looking for, etc. as you use the words repeatedly. >>>

EXERCISE

[4.a] 30-Second Commercial
or Elevator Speech [continued]

Let's get started with your personal commercial:

Step 1: Describe who you are. In a few words, address the request to "tell me about yourself." This should be about your professional function(s) and/or status — not your current or former job title(s). *(Example: Sales management professional)*

Step 2: Now, in up to two sentences, describe your professional history. What was your last position and what were your responsibilities? If you are networking as part of a career transition, you may also use this section to articulate a reason for leaving (or wishing to leave) your last position, as necessary.

Step 3: In a final sentence or two, describe your future focus; what do you want to do next. Or, if you are networking with a prospective client, share your philosophy — explain why you do what you do and why your contact ought to care.

>>>

EXERCISE

[4.a] 30-Second Commercial
or Elevator Speech [continued]

Step 4: Now, put it all together.
You may have to tweak the words a bit to make it flow.

[FIVE]

YOUR
NETWORKING PORTFOLIO

Now, it's time to get organized. You are about to wade into the fray — to meet new people, reconnect with some you already know, make some introductions, establish places to gather for coffee and lunch and the like.

Before we delve into your "must-haves," in terms of your networking portfolio, let's talk about ways NOT to behave as you prepare yourself for networking success. For this, I sought the help of Dr. Tom Denham, a career counselor at the firm Careers in Transition, in Albany, New York. I first saw his lineup of "networking no-no's" in a blog post he published. I knew I couldn't improve on his list of pitfalls to avoid, so with his permission, following are his 50 networking no-no's.

NETWORKING NO-NO'S.

1. Being unprepared or unfocused with your networking objectives

2. Overlooking possible networking connections

3. Overextending with too many targets

4. Being reactive or passive instead of proactive

5. Lacking a name tag

6. Sitting down too early during a networking function or sitting next to people you already know

7. Failing to approach people you don't know at an event

8. Appearing nervous when approaching a potential contact

9. Sending a negative non-verbal message (e.g. arms crossed, poor posture, dressing unprofessionally, wandering eyes, etc.)

10. Giving a weak sound bite or elevator pitch

11. Requesting help with too many things too quickly or strongly

12. Asking for a business card too early

13. Forgetting your business cards!

14. Dominating the conversation by talking, talking, talking

15. Listening selectively and then turning the conversation back to you

16. Sharing your life story

17. Asking questions about areas that seem confidential or controversial

18. Monopolizing other peoples' time

19. Coming across as shallow

20. Latching onto others or clinging to people you already know

21. Acting desperate

22. Asking too many or too few questions

23. Exaggerating or misrepresenting yourself

24. Thinking networking is only about you

25. Failing to find common denominators with others

26. Coming across as inarticulate

27. Selling instead of being a resource to others

28. Being pushy, argumentative, unfriendly, or negative

29. Looking distracted or not fully present

30. Taking, taking, taking

31. Coming across as incompetent or disorganized

32. Showing disinterest

33. Looking like you don't know your stuff

34. Bragging

35. Interrupting

36. Being impulsive

37. Neglecting to reciprocate

38. Failing to deliver on what you promise

39. Forgetting to request a business card!!

40. Focusing on quantity, not quality

41. Over-circulating and trying to talk to everyone

42. Lacking follow-up in a timely manner

43. Expecting immediate payoffs or instant answers

44. Lacking patience in building relationships

45. Forgetting to add new connections to LinkedIn

46. Keeping your network referrers in the dark about your progress

47. Neglecting to nurture your network

48. Turning networking into an afterthought instead of a core priority

49. Failing to reassess the effectiveness of your networking strategy

50. Giving up!!!

Okay—now that you've committed to memory the list of what NOT to do, let's work on what you need to have at your disposal.

ELEVATOR PITCH. Have your elevator pitch always ready to go. Go back to Chapter Four to review your own work and remember to practice!

BUSINESS CARDS. Please, please, please… whatever your purpose in networking, be sure to have a business card (students, I'm talking to you, too). Business cards make it easy to share contact information with others and will help to ensure that you are seen as a true professional. They do not have to be expensive — in fact, go to P.S. Print or Vistaprint.com — that where I get mine. There, you can get very inexpensive and decent quality cards printed in the design of your choice that fits your style and persona. **Caution**: Do NOT go for the free cards… they have a note on the back that says something like "printed at Vistaprint.com" on them and look as cheap as they are… there is a price to "free…." Another great place to order cards is Moo.com — a bit pricier, but the cards are gorgeous and true conversation pieces.

Myself, I have two business cards: One personal card that positions me as a "Marketing, Strategy and General Management" expert, and one professional card as President of Kauffman FastTrac®. Depending on the situation, I hand out the appropriate card.

Oh, and don't forget, business cards have both a front and a back side — some of the coolest, most memorable cards I have seen make good use of the space on the back of the card, too.

EXERCISE

[5.a] Create Your Business Card

Remember, your business card should have some basic information. Not all of these fields will apply to you — you may even have some additional information that you would like to add. If you don't already have a card or would like to consider a design change, take a moment to think through what you plan to include on your business card:

Details to Include on a Business Card	EXAMPLE
Your name	Alana Muller
Title, if you have one	Master Networker
Company name and logo, as appropriate	Coffee Lunch Coffee
Mailing address	P.O. Box 23091 Shawnee Mission, KS 66283-0091
Phone number	☎ 123.456.7890
Email address	✉ Alana@coffeelunchcoffee.com
Website URL	🌐 CoffeeLunchCoffee.com
Twitter handle	🐦 @alanamuller #clcConnect
Facebook URL	facebook.com/coffeelunchcoffee
LinkedIn URL	linkedin.com/in/alanamuller
Blog URL	coffeelunchcoffee.com

Other…
You might also consider putting a phrase or some keywords on the card to give the recipient some idea of what you do. I have even seen people include their company mission. Another idea is to include a QR code to take people to your website or to a video about your company. | Let's Connect!

RÉSUMÉ. You won't always need or want to share your résumé, but when you do, it needs to stand out from everyone else's.

One of my long-time mentors, Eric Morgenstern, who also happens to be a networking genius, once suggested to me that a résumé is like a negligee… it reveals just enough to get the other party interested… Without sounding too risqué (not my intention!), I encourage you to heed that advice! Make sure that your résumé is results focused. There should be plenty of "white space" and the font should be legible. Plus, be sure that it is well written and says what you think it says. Seek feedback from others. It may be necessary to consult a resource on writing a great résumé, or even to hire a professional to help you. However experienced or inexperienced you are, a slam dunk résumé is crucial.

PROFESSIONAL BIO. Whether or not you are employed and whatever your networking objectives, it is important to have a professional bio at the ready. In addition to a bio being a handy tool for introducing yourself to a prospect, the bio can serve other purposes — for example, I find that whenever I am asked to speak at an event or talk with the media, I am asked to share my bio. It can be short and sweet… in this case you can have a short and a long version to accommodate the request. I suggest one at about 200 words and another at about 500 words or one typewritten page, preferably with your photo included. Speaking of which…

PROFESSIONAL HEADSHOT. Having a great, professional photo of yourself is a very useful asset. Not only is it perfect for inclusion on your LinkedIn profile, as we covered in Chapter Two, but it is useful for speaking engagements and the like. If you can afford to do it, have a professional photographer snap a few shots of you — it is a worthwhile investment. By the way, it's probably not a good idea to use a really nice professional photograph of you taken 10 years ago or more!

DO YOUR HOMEWORK. If you have gone to the trouble to reach out to someone to ask for the meeting, please take just a few more minutes to get to know them before you meet them. There is so much information readily available that it would be criminal to not do a little background checking in anticipation of your meeting. Your prospect will be impressed that you bothered and your time together will be more productive because you will know more about the type of information that the prospect might be able to share with you and vice versa.

Sometimes it's a good idea to not openly divulge what you know about the other person — in other words, no need to rattle off a list of facts about them that you acquired through your research! Rather, you may indirectly bring up topics you know will bring a positive reaction from them. For example, if they're from a particular city or state and you have some connection to that location, then indirectly bring it up in the conversation knowing that the person will focus on it, providing you an opportunity to "bond" while discussing a mutually interesting subject. I'm not suggesting any type of inauthenticity; only that the flow of your conversation may be easier if you leverage your new knowledge at strategic times.

[79]

A few resources that I love include:

LinkedIn: We've already talked about the benefits of being on LinkedIn. You can also use it as a resource to review your prospect's contact profile to learn about the companies that he/she has worked at, where he/she went to school, what others are saying about them, how many other contacts they have, blogs they write, etc.

Company website: Be sure to visit the prospect's company website to understand what the firm does, learn about its industry, know what topics/issues it is focused on and, perhaps most importantly, read recent press releases or news articles about the firm.

Your public library: If your local public library is anything like mine, it will have business librarians on staff whose very purpose is to help people like you research information related to business. Plus, most libraries offer free access, via the internet, to a wealth of subscription-only databases and reference information. It is worth taking a mid-afternoon break (maybe between lunch and coffee?) to visit your library and learn about the resources available. (Want to find out who the business decision makers are? One reference database that is awesome is ReferenceUSA; check it out!)

Once you have done your homework — and note, this should not take you too long... maybe 10-15 minutes... you will be able to easily identify areas of common interest, background, experience. These make great conversation igniters and will help to make your meeting more productive.

Brad Douglas
financial services professional and master networker

"Networking is unproductive if it's not a give and take that flows both ways. I recently met with an individual that was networking to find a new job. This person was happy to talk about their needs for the entire 75 minute meeting — and did not ask one single question about me. When the meeting ended, I promised to help them (and did follow through), but as I walked away, I realized this person did not know one thing more about me than they did when I walked in the door other than what I looked like and that I ate an egg sandwich for breakfast! My advice: Do not enter a networking meeting seeking only to help yourself. If you focus emphatically on trying to figure out how you can help the person sitting across from you, you will almost always be rewarded in some way — whether it's later that day or years down the road."

Just in case you feel as if you are drowning in information after reading this far into the book, below is a simple checklist to use as a cheat sheet. I guarantee it will help you feel on top of your game.

NETWORKING PORTFOLIO CHECKLIST

[__] Networking Contacts Matrix
[__] List 1: People I know
[__] List 2: People I want to know
[__] List 3: Companies of interest
[__] List 4: Non-Negotiables
[__] LinkedIn profile
[__] 30-second commercial/Elevator Pitch
[__] Email introduction
[__] Voicemail message
[__] Business cards
[__] Résumé
[__] Professional Bio
[__] Professional Headshot

In closing this chapter, here's a bit of advice from one of the best "connectors" on the planet, Sunny Bates, a legendary influencer who has worked with TED, Kickstarter, Credit Suisse and many other of the most prestigious companies of our time. She is founder of SBA, Sunny Bates Associates. Check out Sunny's website (SunnyBates.com) to get a sense of just how many individuals and companies Sunny has been responsible for helping to get together, and how many fantastic networking and other social events she has dreamed up and coordinated. When interviewed for input for this book, Sunny offered the following advice:

CLC: "What is the value of connection?"
Sunny: "There is nothing more satisfying than seeing a connection between two people flourish. To see mutual needs being fulfilled is a thing of beauty. It thrills me—there is an actual physiological reaction."

CLC: "Please share a story that illuminates how to become an influencer."

Sunny: "An influencer is one who listens and observes. In a world that is so full of people who are broadcasting about themselves, listening, I mean truly listening and paying attention to someone, is a rare occurrence. SO, I like to be the one who really listens. It surprises people because I am such an extrovert and such a big talker, so it is unexpected that I am a great listener, too. How can you possibly influence anyone or anything if you don't really understand, and how can you understand without listening?"

CLC: "What do you do when you walk into a networking event or other gathering where you don't know anyone?"

Sunny: "I look for the shyest or most socially awkward person in the room and I also look for the most outrageously dressed person, or the one who deviates most from the crowd. I'll try my skills with them. Everyone wants to connect — you just have to make the first move."

CLC: "How would you advise a person who's feeling displaced or demoralized because they've lost a job, or a client, and just haven't been able to get moving on the networking front?"

Sunny: "First off, no one should ever be lulled into thinking they will always have a job. Second of all, how can you possibly know what is going on in the world or your industry if you don't keep in contact? You can reach out, you can make it about really connecting, not about just needing a job. And just get over yourself! Everyone has been in a place where they need other people, so it is the height of arrogance to assume you can go along and thrive without others. SO reach out, step by step. Connect with those whom you most respect. Remember that you have to be willing to give something of yourself in order to ask for something. There is a give, and a get. If you make it a one-way channel, it is hardly the foundation on which to build a strong relationship."

Thank you, Sunny! Couldn't have said it better myself!

SIX

NETWORKING:
PEOPLE, PLACES AND THINGS

We've all heard that in real estate it's "location, location, location." Well, in networking the location you select for the venue of a meeting is also important for both for one-on-one meetings and for larger gatherings.

As you already know, the system that works best for me is to meet contacts for coffee in the morning, then have a lunch meeting with a second individual, and have one additional meeting in the afternoon, over coffee. I have my favorite haunts, where I know people and where people know me. I know where I can access wi-fi, where I can go for a quieter meeting vs. one where my guest and I don't mind a livelier vibe. I know where I can go if my contact and I want to spread out. But part of the point is that I like to go where my networking colleague and I can be comfortable, so everything around us is conducive to sharing and connecting.

NETWORK TO AMPLIFY YOUR VOICE

I am a Starbucks fan, and an unabashed admirer of Howard Schultz, Starbuck's CEO. In so many ways, Starbucks has helped foster networking by making it cool to be an entrepreneur, working outside a corporate environment, setting up shop at one of Starbuck's busy tables.

On July 4, 2012, Mr. Schultz wrote an "Open Letter to America" in which he suggested that "As we celebrate all that is great about our country, let's come together and amplify our voices." The letter itself provided an argument and a call to action for Americans to join forces to spur economic recovery through job creation. He reminded us all that if we continue to believe in the greatness of our nation and its long term viability, we must accept a "shared responsibility" to solve our nation's problems. He's right. According to Kauffman Foundation research, the key to economic recovery is through entrepreneurship, which creates new firms, new jobs, and drives the global economy.

So many of Mr. Schultz's messages resonate with me, but in that letter, of particular interest was his use of the word AMPLIFY. That word stayed with me, not only because it is so descriptive in and of itself, but also because that is what networking does. Networking enables us to amplify our work, our voices, our connections. When we are networking, we are helping to build something, we are contributing to an ecosystem of entrepreneurs who cannot exist without each other. When we network in the way and for the reasons discussed here, we are also making a contribution to the economic well-being of our entire country, of our world. That is why I am very proud to consider myself a Networker.

>>>

NETWORK TO AMPLIFY YOUR VOICE [CONTINUED]

A second recent example of how the word amplify has come to occupy a special place in my personal lexicon comes from a fellow by the name of Corey Blake, who is founder and president of Round Table Companies, a storytelling organization. While commenting on the outstanding customer experience provided by Zappos, he said that he likes when companies look deeply into their souls to recognize where real value lives, and he observed: "That's worth amplifying...(Zappos amplifies) that they attract customers who appreciate (service) and staff who love serving. Every company that has these kinds of core values is worth amplifying."

Taking that one step farther, if we are clear about who we are and our purpose in the world, when we are networking, we are amplifying our core values as professionals, and as members of our communities.

[85]

So where are the best places to meet with networking prospects? I will get you started by sharing with you my go-to venues and the characteristics to think about when choosing a location (yes, I pre-plan such things!). Consider geographic vicinity, of course, but also atmosphere, adequate privacy, Wi-Fi availability, how much of a wait there might be, and the like.

Of course, where you will choose to go will vary according to where you live, but it still helps to have some general guidelines. Obviously you won't want to go anywhere that's too quiet (tomb-like) or too noisy, or, frankly, where you'll know too many people who might come over for a "quick" hello and inadvertently interrupt the flow of your networking discussion.

In so many ways, Starbucks and other coffee-shop type environments have helped foster networking by making it cool to be an entrepreneur and to work outside a corporate environment. A coffee shop itself can be a great place not only to meet with your scheduled networking contacts, but also to meet others who are regularly using that site as their "office." Sometimes it feels to me like a kind of club. You can tell after sitting at a table there for a little while who the regulars are.

But I do like to vary my routine, at least a little. It's not good to fall into a rut, even when it comes to networking venues! And when you travel, get suggestions for meeting places from local contacts who are native to the cities you visit, and be sure to keep a list of those venues for future use.

Here are my top picks — my favorite meeting spots — in no particular order:

- **PANERA BREAD®** Panera is a great spot with high efficiency, and given the geographic diversity of my readers, it's easy to suggest as there are more than 7,500 Paneras covering about 40 states. This is a great place to start with coffee in the morning, then work using their free Wi-Fi until 11:30 am, when they shut down the Wi-Fi for lunch. For me, there were (and sometimes still are) three Panera locations that I frequented, where, I noticed, each location seemed to have its own little community of people who've also discovered the comfy atmosphere for meetings. I often saw (see) the same people there day-in/day-out. That sense of belonging, again. Aaah. I love it.

- **McDONALD'S®** Yes, I am one of the millions of people who frequent "Mickey D's". (Anyone who knows me well is aware of my love of Coca-Cola® and the truth is, for my money, McDonald's "makes" the best Coke!®) Anyway, McDonald's stores really are a convenient place to meet— they are everywhere, they are appropriately quiet during mid-morning and mid-afternoon times, and there are plenty of booths for comfort and relative privacy. Many locations offer free Wi-Fi so you can get some computer work done before or after coffee. I probably wouldn't recommend it as a proper lunch venue—too much activity!

- **STARBUCKS.** I've already extolled the virtues of Starbucks, but let me continue on that riff. My husband thinks Starbucks should exit the coffee business to focus on their core competency — atmosphere! They know him at our nearest Starbucks location — he doesn't even have to tell them what he's ordering anymore. The warm cup held lovingly in your hands. The smell of the coffee. The cozy armchairs… it's about a lot more than the coffee itself.

- **LOCAL COFFEE SHOPS.** By the way, while I love Starbucks I equally adore many of the wonderful, locally owned, independent mom 'n pop coffee shops that I also frequent, such as The Roasterie, Aixois, Coffee Girls and a few others. Suffice it to say that coffee shops in general make for good, convenient, reasonably priced meeting spots so long as they have tables and chairs, power outlets, and are spacious enough to give you a little elbow room and privacy for your discussions.

[87]

Any day of the week, I know where to find my friend, Joel Goldman. He is a former attorney and currently the author of several mysteries and thrillers. I guarantee it: He will be at "his table" in the window of Starbucks at 119th & Glenwood in Overland Park, Kansas. It seems he has simply taken up residence! He uses the venue as his platform for writing, for connecting with others, for conducting meetings, for people watching and the like — oh, and, yes, for drinking loads of coffee! It is his virtual office. I think it's great! He is comfortable there, everyone seems to know him, if I need to discuss something with him, I am pretty much assured that he will be there. We all ought to have a go-to place.

My friend, Lindsey Patterson, is owner of Coffee Girls at 75th & Wornall in Kansas City, Missouri. Lindsey shared with me her vision for the shop. She said that she wants to position it as the go-to place for entrepreneurs to meet up, as well as a hub for the neighborhood to gather. Her hope is to encourage people to come and stay — to talk and collaborate with one another, to ask questions and advice of those who have been there before, and, of course, to drink a little coffee, have a nosh and schmooze over freshly made juices. What a beautiful vision! Makes me want to go hang out there.

COFFEE, BUDDY SYSTEM AND OTHER SOURCES OF ENERGY

Speaking of coffee, have you ever been so tired, you simply cannot keep your eyes open? And I don't just mean you need a nap. I mean, do you ever feel trapped in a less-than-virtuous, exhausting cycle you cannot seem to escape? Has there been a time when you wanted to shout: "Go on without me!" Or how about this one: You are working on an important project. There is an expectation that you are on the job around-the-clock. You wake up, and it's still dark outside. You go to your office to work, and work some more. You realize you'd better go home for a bite to eat and a chance to splash some water on your face. You work for another hour, then you finally head home. It's already dark. You eat a little something, work a little more, go to bed, and wake up four hours later. Hit repeat. Ugh. Do you wonder how it's even possible?

My point here is: Do you have staying power? Do you have what it takes to go the distance? Can you see a light at the end of the tunnel? Are you motivated to reach that light? Sure, take a break if you must when you start to feel a little bit of networking fatigue. But, then, try picking yourself up by injecting a little "intro savvy" into your routine.

INTRO SAVVY

In Chapter Five, I shared Sunny Bates' remarks about the charge she gets from seeing a networking relationship blossom between two people who she had a hand in connecting. It can provide a giant boost of energy to both the connected and to the connector. It is vitally important to be both connected and a connector, in other words, to request and receive introductions to new people, on the one hand, and on the other, to introduce your contacts to each other.

With special thanks to my friend Ken Glickstein, I offer this piece of advice on the etiquette of serving as a connector, earning admiration, allegiance and respect, and avoiding networking faux pas. There are countless ways to make an introduction—some good; others, not so much.

Let's take each in turn.

For these examples, let's name our characters. First, there is Jane. Jane is well connected and knows both Keisha and Lauren. Keisha asks Jane for an introduction to Lauren. Jane agrees to make the introduction. Here's how the scenarios could play themselves out:

BAD. Let's just get this one out of the way. Jane recently met Lauren at a benefit luncheon. They happened to be seated at the same table, exchanged business cards, but had very little meaningful conversation. In fact, Jane is unsure that Lauren will even remember her. As such, Jane reluctantly gives Lauren's contact details to Keisha with the caveat that she not mention that she received her name, number and email address from Jane. Basically, Keisha is making a cold call — there is no warmth or familiarity to contacting someone out of the blue. She might as well have looked up Lauren's number on Google! This is cold, and very uncool. Unless you are willing to allow "Keisha" to use your name as a reference, don't give out "Lauren's" contact information. Period. It is poor form and shows little imagination!

[89]

GOOD. Jane gives Lauren's contact details (phone number, email address, maybe her company and title, too) to Keisha and says, "Be sure to tell Lauren that I suggested you connect with her." OK. Well, this works and frankly, I've employed this tactic many times. That said, it is by far the laziest of the approaches to introductions! It accomplishes the initial goal in terms of Jane checking the box for having given Keisha the information and Keisha does, indeed, now have a way to contact Lauren. However, Keisha is still out there flying solo. Lauren is less likely to take Keisha's call or open her email since she doesn't recognize Keisha's name than she would be if the initial outreach came directly from Jane herself.

BETTER. What would be better is if Jane sent a mutual introduction to both Keisha and Lauren with some context for why they should connect. This is my favorite approach to making introductions. It is only slightly more time consuming than GOOD and shows some genuine effort on my part. I start with something in the subject line like, "Introduction: Lauren/Keisha," then open my message with "Lauren — Meet Keisha. Keisha — Meet Lauren." From there, I provide two or three sentences about each of Lauren and Keisha to give them some understanding for who the other person is, what they do and a high level reason for why I think they should meet. I also share phone numbers and email addresses. I close with, "I will leave it to the two of you to connect." In this scenario, Jane still checked the box, but she put forth a bit more effort by personally facilitating the introduction, made it more comfortable for both parties, justified why Lauren ought to give Keisha the time of day and helped to ensure that Lauren and Keisha will actually connect. Good job, Jane. Good job so long as you are certain that Lauren won't mind that you have shared her contact details with someone she doesn't know. CAUTION: If you have any inkling at all that Lauren might care or if you don't know Lauren well enough to know, you might consider a higher touch approach to the introduction.

BEST. If Jane really wanted to show Lauren the consideration and respect that I know she has for her, she would take Keisha's request under advisement. From there, she would phone Lauren or send her a direct, private email message requesting permission to share her contact information with Keisha. Indeed, this approach takes a lot more time. However, once permission is granted, Keisha is assured of actually connecting with Lauren since Lauren will be expecting her call or email. I suppose it is possible that Lauren will decline Jane's request; if she does, Jane can respond to Keisha's inquiry by indicating that she is unable to share Lauren's information, but can suggest another of her contacts that Keisha could connect with and who can offer similar guidance and advice as an alternative.

When he contacted me about this topic, Ken shared that he tends toward GOOD when he knows the "Lauren" in our scenarios really well and feels certain that she won't mind him giving out her contact information (so long as Keisha makes note of Ken's reference when he reaches out to Lauren). Ken went on to say that he tends toward BETTER when he knows Lauren less well. He says that he is still thoughtful about whom and to whom he makes introductions. However, recently, after a BETTER introduction, Ken received a polite response from Lauren with a request to, in the future, seek her permission first before sharing her contact details. Ouch!

What I appreciated most about Ken's message is the following:

"I realize now that both of my approaches [GOOD and BETTER] are rather presumptive. Both approaches, of course, assume that every target in my contact database will be willing to, at a minimum, spend 20 minutes speaking with any networker [like Keisha] that I believe justifies an introduction. I attempt to counter this by being very judicious in identifying targets [like Lauren] and by limiting the number of times I use anybody as a target over a given period of time. I suspect I have adopted these approaches because: (i) at a minimum, I am generally willing to spend 20 minutes on a phone conversation with anyone that one of my contacts thinks I can be of assistance to, and (ii) I am a little bit lazy and would rather not go through a two-step process to facilitate the intro."

Upon further reflection, Ken noted that if he were to employ BEST more frequently, he might, over time, be able to categorize targets into those that prefer GOOD vs. BETTER vs. BEST. Great observation and idea, Ken! I couldn't agree more and I, too, have struggled with this issue.

Let's take our scenarios one more round…

BESTEST. (I know, "bestest" ain't a word… go with me on this one.) Better than BEST might be if Jane not only sought and received Lauren's consent to share her contact details with Keisha, but offered to organize coffee or lunch among the three of them. In that way, Jane could, herself, enjoy a touch point with each of Keisha and Lauren, but she should also help to guide the discussion so that Keisha and Lauren were made to feel comfortable with one another.

Of GOOD, BETTER, BEST and/ or BESTEST, which approach do you prefer to take when making introductions? When receiving introductions? Do you have another approach to share?

> *My mom, Charlene Muller, called me recently and exclaimed, "One of my contacts just took a page right out of your blog!" She went on to relay a conversation and follow up email she received from a former client. The client, we'll call him "Shawn," called and asked, "Are you fully locked in to using just one loan officer to assist your real estate clients?" When she told him that she was open to meeting others, he said, "I met a young woman who does lending work. She is excellent at her job — very committed, hard-working and concerned for the welfare of her clients. In fact, she reminds me of you, Charlene. I would like to introduce the two of you." My mom, of course, agreed to the introduction. What happened next, however, surprised her. The next day, she received an email from Shawn inviting her for tea at his office the following week to meet the loan officer. Yep, a BESTEST introduction! I suspect that future transactions are likely between my mom and the woman that Shawn introduced to her.*
>
> *High touch, high reward.*

Recently, I had coffee with a friend who is on the job market. He's looking at all kinds of opportunities, doing his own project work on the side, networking in between. Sure, he has moments of pure frustration, and no doubt desolation. He's concerned that his professional life is temporarily off balance. He wonders what toll all of the uncertainty will have on his family. He takes a deep breath. He keeps going. He has staying power. I, for one, am impressed by his stick-to-itiveness. He has the right attitude. He is absolutely convinced that things will level out eventually, but he is not just rolling with it. He is seizing every possible opportunity to steer his destiny in the direction he chooses. Networking is his weapon of choice.

BUDDY SYSTEM

That brings to me to another extremely useful, at times life-saving networking tool, and that is **the buddy system**. Since networking is a contact sport, make it a team sport.

When I first started toying with the idea of setting out on my own, I signed up for TheLadders; it's a membership driven jobs board that aims to connect job seekers with relevant opportunities. In addition to its work as a matchmaker, TheLadders puts out weekly e-blasts and newsletters with tips and advice for interviewing, resume writing, working with recruiters and the like. One article (well, only a few sentences, really), published on January 22, 2008, has stuck with me all these years:

"Buddy up during your job search! Having a friend who is also seeking employment can provide great benefits to both parties involved. You and your buddy can express similar concerns, boost each other's morale, and empathize with one another as you share advice and success."
— Barbara Safani, Career Solvers

My #1 networking buddy was Scott Carson (who, by the way, is now a member of my team at Kauffman FastTrac® — he is doing amazing work!). Truly, Scott is the best networker I know. I remain grateful to him for teaching me about effective networking and for supporting me in the true spirit of partnership. Each of you should find a networking buddy — hopefully one like Scott.

Here's the deal... during our first discussion about potentially "buddying up," Scott opened his virtual Rolodex (aka, Blackberry) to me and started sharing names and contact details for several potential networking prospects.

>>>

BUDDY SYSTEM [CONTINUED]

He even seemed to have a handle on my networking calendar better than I did; each time I finished up coffee, lunch or coffee, I would get a call or an email from Scott asking how my meeting went — he'd ask about the person by name, what I learned about the company, who else they connected me with, etc… it was amazing. Beyond that, each time he finished a networking discussion himself, he'd proactively tell me about the highs and lows and, when appropriate, he'd suggest that I meet with the person next! Oh, there was certainly quid pro quo… I shared a lot of contacts with Scott, too, but he was the one who showed me by example the meaning of teamwork in terms of networking. And, just to add to the idol worship, you need to know that Scott landed a position a few weeks before I did, but he didn't forget about his little networking buddy… he contacted me several times per week just to check in and see how my networking was going and, of course, to give me more contact prospects. Wow!

Oh, yes, there was even one time when Scott and I inadvertently ended up in contention for the same gig. And, yes, it was awkward… I suggest you avoid that with your buddy. But Scott and I both seemed to handle it like adults and, to this day, we are friends and he will forever set the standard in my mind for the ideal networking buddy.

Scott had this to say about the approach we took to support one another:

For me, our approach created instant accountability. You and I were very focused on re-connecting to our local business community, not easy when I'd been away for 20 years and your base of connections was outside the area. We were supportive of each other, very competitive, and cheerleaders at times, but, most importantly, genuine in our focus to help each other make that next connection. I believe we both knew that, in the end, no matter who landed his/her next gig first, it was a victory for both of us. We always had the other person's best interest in mind throughout. That mindset by both 'buddies,' drives successful networking every time. There wasn't any doubt that with this approach we would be successful.

Take this away for yourself:

- Don't go it alone.

- Find a friend, a networking buddy, to partner with during the networking process.

- Rely on that buddy, share information about when things go well and when they go less well. Ask for feedback. Heed his/her advice.

- Be there for your buddy — even after one of you lands a position.

Networking can offer true solace during times of dislocation and uncertainty. It can bring you a sense of belonging and inspire you. It can help perk you up when you are feeling down, or offer a sense of hope that, yes, change is possible. But try not to substitute networking for therapy. People like to be around others who are enthusiastic, exude high energy and display esprit for whatever it is they are engaged in. As you seek out others in a networking capacity, remember to bring your most positive self to the table. A glass-half-full attitude will win you more influence and keep you at top of mind much more readily than a ho-hum, glass-half-empty sort of approach. I'm not suggesting that you gloss over areas of concern or act in an inauthentic manner. Rather, I'm suggesting that your positive outlook will bring an aura of hope, happiness, excitement that will leave your networking contacts eager for more interaction with you. Smile — often!

EXERCISE

[6.a] Your Key Contacts

Here is something you might share with your regular networking buddy, a project you can help each other contribute to and regularly maintain. I recently read something interesting in the *Harvard Business Review*, by Kellogg School of Management Professor Brian Uzzi and Shannon Dunlap, about a suggested networking exercise that is really fun and useful in helping chart the source of your most meaningful networking contacts. They suggest that you write down who you think are your key contacts. Reflect on how you first met them and on a worksheet, note in the center column who initially introduced you to that contact. If you met the person yourself, write "me." The worksheet will tell a story. It will chart who are the "brokers" in your network, and illuminate the networking process you utilized to connect with those people. A pattern will begin to emerge, one you can use as a template to follow again and again.

Name Of Contact	Who Introduced Me To The Contact?	To Whom Have I Introduced The Contact?
Example: Nancy	Ming	Chloe, Sunil, Avi
Example: Eric	Me	Munro, Stephanie, Kelly
Example: Tyshon	Iliana	Quincy, Maya
Example: Simon	Betsy	Noah
Example: Karen	Betsy	Talia, Beth, Dana
1.		
2.		
3.		
4.		
5.		
6.		
7.		
8.		
9.		
10.		

Source: Adapted from "How to Build Your Network," by Brian Uzzi and Shannon Dunlap. *Harvard Business Review*, December 2005.

[SEVEN]

STEP OUTSIDE
YOUR COMFORT ZONE

Some of the best networkers out there not only look around them — at their communities and ecosystems — for inspiration and to size up where they fit within them, but are also adept at turning apparent lemons into lemonade. In this chapter, we will explore the best ways of taking your one-on-one networking skills and bringing them to larger networking events. Events where you may have to do something really brave — introduce yourself to strangers.

To get us started, let me share a story about one of the gurus of social networking, Media Bistro founder, Laurel Touby. Laurel offers an excellent example of turning lemons into lemonade. She took her feeling of displacement and isolation and converted it into one of the most powerful networks in the United States.

Laurel came to New York City after college dreaming of becoming a writer. She thought of her career as something to be nurtured and was building a database of people as she made new contacts. She says she even went as far as to send Valentine's Day cards to new contacts as a follow-up. She got a few magazine staff jobs here and there, but nothing really clicked, and she was forced to go back to freelancing. Finding freelance writing to be a lonely profession and spending way too much time alone in her apartment, she started going out during the day to work out of local cafes (coffee??).

One day she met a fellow freelancer, a guy who wrote for the *Village Voice*. They commiserated over the isolation of the freelancer's life, and he suggested they throw a cocktail party together.

Laurel invited five friends, and her counterpart invited another five. They found that they were energized by the event, and decided to host regular events, "salons," to which they would invite select people from the media world. The salons quickly became popular, and someone suggested Laurel launch a website.

[98]

For her website, she had the idea to ask companies with job openings to post the available positions on the site and pay her if the postings resulted in job applicants. Bottom line: Laurel ended up selling the company for $23 million dollars and as the hostess of one of the most successful salon series in the country, she will never be lonely again.

I mention Laurel because like so many successful entrepreneurs the cornerstone of her entire brand is networking. She didn't start out thinking: Let me monetize my network and sell it for a lot of money. Rather, she proceeded very authentically, organically, out of necessity, to connect with others in professional situations comparable to hers. One contact led to another, and the rest is history. And, while not every one of us will build networks that will translate into multi-million dollar ventures like Media Bistro, every single one of us has the capacity to create a network, be part of a larger ecosystem that we regularly contribute to, and that supports and feeds us.

Here are some excerpts from an interview with Laurel conducted exclusively for this book:

CLC: "How would you describe networking?

Laurel: "Networking is really about connecting. It is not about neediness. Don't go into networking feeling needy. If you feel needy, reassess yourself and decide YOU'RE NOT! There should never be a power imbalance, no matter how powerful the person on the other side of the table is. That doesn't mean you don't have to sometimes tailor your approach to take age or gender into account, and it doesn't mean you're disrespecting them, but it's important to try and treat the person as a peer. Whenever I've gone up to someone I admire and said 'I admire you!' their first reaction was to escape. Powerful people enjoy connecting with peers."

CLC: "If someone seems to be talking at you, and not necessarily listening to you or asking what you are looking for, what do you suggest?"

Laurel: "Gently begin inserting yourself into the conversation at first with questions about them."

CLC: "That may be an abstract concept for some. Can you provide an example of inserting yourself into the conversation?"

Laurel: "I was at a dinner party and was seated next to a well-known architect in his sixties. For the first fifteen minutes or so all he did was talk about himself. Occasionally, I asked him questions about himself, but he didn't ask one question about me. Now, I did the wrong thing. I got aggressive. I said: 'We've spoken for fifteen minutes and you haven't asked me one question about myself.' That stopped him dead in his tracks. I told him about my business and described some of my accomplishments, including how I'd sold Media Bistro for millions of dollars. And then I said: 'Now I'm looking to get into venture capital. How can I help YOU?' Because I did it with a smile and some humor, it turned out fine, and I got my point across, though I wouldn't recommend handling the situation that way. But the point is that sometimes people are accustomed to performing, not paying attention. **Realize who your audience is, but don't get offended if they aren't asking you questions. Instead, gently steer the conversation in the direction that suits your topic. Women especially too often end up deferring, or submitting, instead of asserting themselves.**"

CLC: "Often, people get anxious, nervous or antsy before attending a large networking event. Any advice?"

Laurel: "It's much more important to go into the room to connect emotionally, or intellectually. Your goal shouldn't be about 'networking,' it should be about connecting. If you are intimidated, remember to go to your lowest common denominator, which is: You're both human. We're all struggling in our own ways.

"If you are feeling down, or if your current professional status is 'unemployed,' or if an awkward question about your status arises and you get flustered, being honest, e.g. 'I don't know why I haven't found a new job yet.' That said, keep it light, say the truth, but with a little humor. At the end of the day, if you follow this advice, people will leave the conversation thinking: I bet it's not even true that he or she has been out of work. They're too charming and funny for that to be true!"

Thank you, Laurel, for that great mini-workshop!

THE BIG EVENT

Now that we are onto the topic of networking in the context of large events or "meet-ups," we must spend some time getting ready. Not everyone who is good at one-on-one networking is naturally good at or likes going out to networking functions where they will likely be walking into a room filled with strangers. If you dread these events, try and remind yourself that not only are they often professionally useful, they can also be fun if approached the right way. And who knows? You might make a new friend or two.

So how should you approach networking events to get the most bang for your buck, even if you are one of those people who dread them?

Can't think of what to say...

- "So, tell me about yourself..." Have a great five second answer! Also have great 10, 20 and 30 second answers.

- "How are you?" Don't say, "fine." Instead, pick a word or phrase that is uniquely yours. You could say, "Fabulous!" or "Terrific!" or "Great!" Just don't say, "Fine." Mine is "Awesome!" Follow it up with one sentence that explains why things are so "Outstanding!" such as, "I just had the best adventure with my son," or "We just launched a fabulous initiative at work that is being very well received by our customers."

- At a networking event...

  - Take the name of a great new restaurant, a great movie, a cool new attraction in your city to share with people.

  - Start the conversation with, "what a great tie!" or "have you heard this speaker before?"

  - If you are sitting with a group at a luncheon, dinner event or awards banquet, make a point of getting up and going around to everyone at the table. Shake their hand and say hello; you'd be surprised at how infrequently people do this — it will get you noticed... in a good way!

Step one is to carefully select the events you choose to attend. Don't feel compelled to be at every event to which you're invited. I like to think about networking events in the following terms:

- Why should I attend this event?

- What is the purpose of attending? Am I seeking new referrals or new contacts for my existing professional network?

- Is this the sort of gathering where I should be seen, and where I will meet connectors and influencers? If so, would it be good for building my profile?

- Am I looking for the support of my peer group, or to collect as much information as possible about my industry or my community?

- Does it just sound like a cool event that I could attend with a friend, and we'd both have a great time?

Once you've figured out your intention for attending the event or meet-up and assessed whether the event actually offers what you are looking for, put it on your calendar! If you are nervous about attending alone, ask a friend who also might get something out of participation in the event to join you. But if you do go with someone, be sure you don't just stand in a corner together all night. Fan out, reach out, and connect.

I often find large networking events to be quite awkward. When I do attend, I always try to remind myself that I am not the only person in the room who is feeling awkward or self-conscious. I am probably not even in the minority. There are some very good tips out there on how to get past your shyness and plunge right in. Here is some advice from Business and Productivity Coach, Carrie Greene, of CarrieThru.com:

1. *Rescue someone*.

   There is always going to be someone in the room besides you who is feeling a little tentative in a large networking gathering. Sometimes you can even spot them just by looking around. Why not identify a person who looks like they might welcome a friendly face and go over and introduce yourself? Don't spend too much time thinking about what you're going to say. Instead, just compliment them on the jacket they are wearing or on their earrings. Start with a compliment and take the time to learn about them.

2. *Relax*.

   Don't try too hard at impressing the person you are talking to. Be yourself. Don't "hard sell."

3. *Networking events are not competitions*.

   It's not about meeting as many people as you can meet in the course of the hour or so you are there. It's about making a few real connections, ones you can build on.

4. *Don't neglect the follow-up*.

   Too often, people exchange cards or contact information, and then do nothing with it. Write a nice thank-you note saying you were glad to make a new acquaintance. Suggest another meeting. But don't waste the contact.

5. *Show up… consistently*.

   One way to avoid feeling like a stranger in a strange land at networking events is to attend the same events regularly. You will begin to feel like you belong, and as we know, that's a great feeling.

Once you have overcome some of the psychological hurdles of successfully participating in social networking events you can really get down to business. To that end, I suggest you "fish where the fish are," in other words, go in prepared to connect with people you'd like to meet but might not otherwise have access to. Here is my playbook for maximizing large event networking:

1. ***Go in prepared.***

   Once you know about an event and have committed to attending, set a goal. Is there one person (or two? or more?) whom you believe might be there? If so, seek out that individual for a simple introduction. Also, have some valuable information on the tip of your tongue that can be shared with anyone you come in contact with, such as the name of a great handyman or a fabulous new restaurant, the kind of info that is useful fodder for engaging in a discussion with people you may be meeting for the first time. The few minutes that you spend preparing for these events will pay dividends.

2. ***Look at the event as an invitation to join the inner circle.***

   One of my most loyal blog supporters is my childhood friend, Jack. He's a law professor at the University of Southern California who has been promoting my blog to his students and colleagues. He tells me that while networking can be challenging for graduate students, with a little effort, it can be done, especially if they take the Coffee-Lunch-Coffee structure and adapt it for their fields of study and/or professional interests. He uses the example of the law firm recruiting process, which is highly routinized and leaves little room for networking as a tool for job seekers. That said, he suggests that law students attending continuing education and related networking events that lawyers go to, which often have reduced or even free admission for law students. There, the students can meet and get to know people in their industry as a means of getting into the business. The same holds true whether you are a law student, a financial planner, a corporate executive, a freelance writer, or a sales rep. Don't know where to look for networking events? Start with your local Chamber of Commerce or Rotary Club. Find a relevant industry trade or special interest organization for your industry, or your desired customers' industries. Ask someone you admire which events they attend... perhaps even ask if you can accompany them next time.

3. *Once you are on the scene*...

My friend and mentor, Eric Morgenstern of Morningstar Communications, does a great talk on tips for networking events. The entire list follows at the end of the chapter, but I can't resist pointing out a few of my favorites. The first is: Wear a name tag and affix it on your right hand side lapel. That makes it easier for your contacts to discreetly recall (and later remember) your name when they go to shake your hand. A second tip that Eric shares is: If you want to make sure that you get to see the people you want to see and talk with, stand near the food and/or bar. Everyone seeks out food and drink, right? So why not stake out your position there? Eric reminds us, however, not to stand in front of the food—just near it!

4. *What do you Share and Take Away?*

I recommend the following: at a networking event, your goal should be to identify and connect with a few key contacts. The goal is not to come home with as many business cards as possible, but to come away with cards from a few people with whom you want to follow up. And by the way, don't forget your business cards, and to exchange them with your contacts. But do restrict that to cards only—no resumes, business plans or other marketing collateral. (That can come later.)

Eric M. Morgenstern

President and CEO, Morningstar Communications is a master networker.

Eric provides the following ten steps for achieving success at networking events and mixers:

1. *Nametag on the right*

   Place your nametag on your right lapel or side. That way, it is easier for your contacts to discreetly recall (and later, remember) your name when they go to shake your hand.

2. *Restate Their Name*

   When you are first introduced, say the person's name right back to them. Not only will this ensure you got it right, you have a much greater likelihood of remembering it. Using a person's name also personalizes the conversation.

3. *Share / Get*

   Before you go to any networking event, say to yourself, "this is something I'd like to share; this is something I'd like to get." A great new store or restaurant… perhaps a supplier… non-business suggestions work well. Effective networking is both give and take.

4. *"Questions are the creative acts of intelligence"*

   This quote, from Einstein, plays very well in networking. Asking smart, open-ended questions gets the person talking. Put on your "reporter" hat and listen intently, and the conversation will easily evolve.

5. *The early bird catches the connections*

   Arrive early so you can become acclimated to the environment. You'll have some of your best conversations when the room isn't quite as crowded. >>>

6. *Stand by the food / bar*

The attendees will come by you, and it will be easy to find things to discuss.

7. *Think quality vs. quantity*

Strive for making just one or two good conversations that lead to subsequent discussions. This is worth much more than a pocket full of business cards without any real connections.

8. *Write on business cards*

As soon as your conversation ends, scribble a few notes on the back of their card. It will jog your memory for follow-up.

9. *It's not who you know; it's who knows you*

Be memorable, in a good way. Help the people you meet remember you by asking great questions, telling a poignant story, or following up in an appropriate manner.

10. *Don't say "fine"*

When a stranger asks, "How are you?" You're not fine. Nobody's fine. Give a real answer that's memorable and magnetic. Something like, "Excellent." Or "I'm doing great… how are you today?"

And a bonus tip…

11. *The power of a hand-written note*

The single best way to leave a positive and memorable impression is simply a brief, hand-written thank you note sent within 24 hours after the contact.

Lessons Learned
Michele Markey, Entrepreneur, VP — Kauffman FastTrac®

Let me start by saying I love networking. I love meeting new people and learning about their work, background, experiences and life passions. It is always interesting to me and I rarely leave a networking experience sorry for investing the time. My perspective is that networking is a sampling of the various walks of life — It is always an experience, so bring it on! Variety, truly, is the spice of life.

For me the biggest challenge/lesson learned over the years has been to understand and gain clarity around the objective of networking. I have come to understand that it is not about collecting business cards or building an impressive rolodex. It is also not simply to have friendly chit chat with a broad swath of people (although great for weddings and college reunions!). Instead, great networking — truly powerful networking — is really about establishing a different level of connection; something I call "intentional networking."

Intentional networking is about building an infrastructure of contacts/relationships with those offering a diversity of skills, representing various industries, backgrounds and knowledge bases — a collection of resources and talent that can help one another, leveraging the power of many over one. At first blush expending so much time and effort developing a network might seem frivolous especially as calendars are packed and schedules are stretched. But the reality is, intentional networking is as much about strategy as building a marketing plan or sketching out your financials. Business is about people. Having a solid network that can be successfully leveraged is key — whether looking for funding sources, searching for talent for your board or even seeking mentors, having a robust network is essential to business and personal success.

To meet new people, I go to events, conferences, business meetings, church functions, social situations, etc. and walk in willing to engage with others. Too often, people spend time telling their own story or, on the opposite extreme, sitting quietly never engaging with others. They stay within their comfort zones because it would be "awkward" to make an overture. The best networking advice I could offer is to go into all situations with an open heart and an open mind — you never know who you will meet. You must be willing actively participate in conversation. Make the effort, initiate conversation with someone you don't know. It may be uncomfortable at first but you will be amazed at how open others will be to your overture.

EIGHT

THE NETWORKING MASTER CLASS

As I was contemplating what to offer you in this chapter, I got to thinking about the definition of "mastery." Albert Einstein observed that, "Only one who devotes himself to a cause with his whole strength and soul can be a true master. For this reason, mastery demands all of a person."

Mastery is about developing full command of a subject, about consummate skill.

When you have truly mastered a subject, you can converse about it, think about it, and operate within it, with ease. Mastery enables you to feel confident and in the zone. But true masters know that they are never done learning or refining their skills. They eagerly pursue information, keep learning and continue working so they can remain on top of their games.

Throughout this book you have been introduced to some of the people I consider to be master networkers. Some of those people are extremely well-known, with bestselling books or famous clients to their credit, while others keep a lower profile, but are nonetheless invaluable sources of wisdom.

By some, I am considered a master networker. However, I think of myself as more of a student, always learning, and always wanting to share and discuss what I've learned with those around me. That's why I started my blog, and why I wrote this book. However, the blog and book are also efforts to further expand my network, and make connections with readers I might not otherwise have met. In a way, writing this book is the ultimate expression of networking — of connecting with others.

My home town of Kansas City recently had the honor of hosting Major League Baseball's All Star Game for the first time since 1973. What does that have to do with networking mastery? I'm getting to that... And by the way, what is the All Star Game if not an opportunity for true baseball masters to get together to really show off their stuff, and to mingle (network) with each other?

In preparation for the game, countless hours were spent not only by the players and their coaches, but also by the grounds crews, catering staff, retailers, city planners, journalists, photographers, etc. They worked to get ready for the week, to make sure everyone had done their homework, and, of course, to ensure that Kansas City itself was shown to its best advantage. Everyone put their expertise to the test and it made for a fantastic show, whether you are an American League fan, a National League fan, or just a fan of people getting together to celebrate a great American tradition. Here's the point — for all of those who contributed to bringing off the event in such grand fashion, their work did not start the day it was announced that the game would be held in Kansas City, and it certainly didn't begin on the day of the game. The expertise(s) of those who came together for that event began, for each and every individual, many years ago, and no doubt they have each continued to hone their skills over time, perhaps even on a daily basis.

One concept that I really buy into is that we should all think of ourselves as lifelong learners. Are you a person who constantly and consistently strives to acquire new and advanced knowledge and information? That is something I seek to do—to continually expand my mind for the rest of my days.

By contrast, I once had a manager who told me that because they already had an MBA and had risen through the corporate ranks to a relatively senior position, they no longer required professional development. I remember feeling sad for this individual — how boring to think that the remainder of their long career path would be guided by "no additional development necessary." To boot, and I'm certain not coincidentally, this person was one of the least effective managers I've ever encountered, and would have benefited greatly from a little professional improvement!

I suspect we've all met someone who proudly says, "I have 17 years of experience." Then, once we get to know him/her, we realize they have one year's worth of experience that they've repeated 16 more times!

A friend told me not long ago that after a bit of turnover among her employees, her boss recommended that she take a management class that the company would subsidize. At first she was insulted. After all, she was already a VP and had successfully headed a department for years. But the more she reflected on it, the more she realized that if the company was willing to invest in her skills, she should consider herself lucky! Even a veteran manager can get stale, and need a refresher course.

Turns out, we're never fully cooked, folks! There is always more that we can do to learn, to expand our knowledge, to improve our prowess at whatever task is at hand. Which, of course, holds true for networking.

I figure that in the first half of this year alone, I clocked between 250-500 hours of networking time. That's morning and afternoon coffee meetings, lunch meetings, networking events, conferences and the like.

Assuming I keep up the same pace for the remainder of the year, let's say, on average, I get in about 750 networking hours. Now, let's assume that I had a similar average number of hours in each of the years since I really began networking in earnest. That's about 3,500 networking hours. Seem like a lot? Well, perhaps it is a good start, but, truly, that ain't nothin'!

In his 2008 book *Outliers: The Story of Success*, author Malcolm Gladwell asserts that for an individual to attain expert status in any given topic, he or she must spend at least 10,000 hours practicing and developing his/her proficiency. This 10,000-Hour Rule is described in the context of talents such as those of The Beatles, who performed live in Hamburg, Germany more than 1,200 times from 1960 to 1964, racking up more than 10,000 hours of play time — not only enabling John, Paul, George and Ringo to become "experts" in their field (and we know how that turned out), but also helping them to really craft a sound that was

[112] uniquely theirs—and the rest is history.

You too, can be a life-long learner.

Though you are already well-connected, well-thought of, well-liked, and/or well-known—that doesn't mean you should leave "well" enough alone. We each possess the capacity to continue to expand our minds and knowledge beyond where we currently are. If you have said "If I'd only known then what I know now," as often as I have, I don't have to convince you that there is more to be gained through new experiences and learning, and through building new relationships.

So here's my challenge to you: Get out of your comfort zone. Identify a group, an industry, a type of individual with whom you don't currently have many points of contact, but would complement your current network or business or hobby. Next, decide to build out your network!

A few months ago, Scott Carson, the networking buddy I introduced you to in Chapter Six, reconnected with his fraternity brother, Brad. After doing so, he suggested that I get to know this fellow — not for any reason in particular, but just because he thought we could add value to each other in some way. Of course, I met with Brad and wouldn't you know it? He and I hit it off right away! We discovered not only that we share a love of networking and have many contacts in common, but also that we each knew numerous other new contacts we each could share with the other. From my perspective, there was value creation happening right before my eyes! Brad provided me with warm introductions to three new people: Frank, Serri and Nate — I've already met with each of them and, sure enough, we are now helping to build bridges for one another. Will all this effort and these connections actually lead to something beneficial? Based on my experience, and that of many thousands of other networkers, I know that it will. Do I know when? *No.* Do I know which one of us will realize some tangible benefit? *No.* However, will one or all of us benefit in some tangible way? *You bet.*

Gather new knowledge.

We have talked about life-long learning. One of the best ways to advance this knowledge is by learning from others around you. Pick a topic — any topic — that you want to learn more about and find out who in your network can assist. Have a great new camera but unsure how to decode F-stops and aperture settings? Ask a contact who is a great photographer for a crash course. Want to learn how to decorate a cake? Ask a friend to join you for such a class. Is your goal to climb a 14,000 peak or two? Find out who in your community is collecting 14Ks and ask for some pointers. What a great way to connect with someone. People love to talk about the things they know and understand. Give them the chance. You'll learn, they'll smile.

Another terrific way to bolster your knowledge about a number of topics is via TED Talks (ted.com). TED is a nonprofit organization with the moniker, "Ideas Worth Spreading." Like the Medici family of Renaissance Italy, TED was originally organized to bring together people from a variety of disciplines, in TED's case: Technology, Entertainment and Design. What started as a single conference held for an exclusive audience has blossomed into a movement. With thousands of videos from a diverse variety of people from all over the world on countless topics, I urge you to discover your own favorite TED talks (mine are plentiful and include — among others — talks from Simon Sinek, Matt Cutts, Sheryl Sandberg, Jill Bolte Taylor, Salman Kahn, Derek Sivers... the list goes on). They are poignant, funny, emotional, controversial, enlightening, inspiring... and I love to talk about them with others who have experienced them, too. Guaranteed — if you want something to talk about with your contacts, watch a TED Talk or two. I dare you not to be inspired and smarter as a result.

I would also be remiss — as a blogger myself — if I didn't direct you to get engaged in blogs. You may choose to blog and/or to read others' blogs. Either way, you will gain new insight on topics ranging from networking to organic foods to child rearing to politics to entrepreneurship to women's issues to everything in between and beyond! A great place to start is by finding a few blogs to follow — visit WordPress.com or BlogHer.com to begin your blog journey.

Lead with, "How can I help you?"

We've talked a lot about networking being a two-way street. One should not enter a networking engagement poised to ask for something. A more refined, more elegant approach to networking is to go in singularly focused on how you can help your contact. Of course, this takes finesse and sometimes takes some getting used to, as well as a genuine desire to help. By way of example, every time I see super networker Eric Morgenstern, he looks right at me and asks, "What can I do to help you?" Many others do, too. For them, "What can I do to help you?" is an authentic, heart-felt, sincere question that is part of each of these individuals' standard vernacular. Whenever this happens, I tend to blush (back to those non-verbal signals we need to get under control) — almost ashamed that I didn't think to ask them first what I could do to help them!

You may be thinking to yourself, "I'm way too busy trying to keep my head above water to be out there lending a hand to others who are doing just fine." You don't have time to provide for someone else, right? Wrong! The more adept you are at networking, the more time you will actually create for yourself because your contacts will line up to help you when you need something! Each time you provide a favor, each time you make an introduction, each time you offer a small gift (e.g. an interesting article, the name of a great new restaurant, a movie review), you are building social capital with your contacts. The quid pro quo nature of great networking will continue to pay you back in ways unimagined.

It's not "networking," it's "relationship building."
Focus on nurturing those relationships.

Continuing with advice received recently from new contacts in my network, Frank Bonura, "The Connecter" and Executive Agent, had this to say about his perspective on making contacts:

> *"The only time I refer to 'networking' or 'network' is when I describe the differences between those terms and a relationship base. I encourage everyone I encounter not to pursue 'networking,' but to focus on 'relationships.' Networking is just 'card swapping.' And, if you are not nurturing your relationships, you do not possess a relationship base; in that case you have only a network of strangers."*

Frank takes a hard line on this topic — truth told, I am not so caught up in the specific vernacular, but I agree that it is at least as important to manage and maintain your present, strong network as it is to continue to build it out through additional connections. Frank tells me that the way that he does this is that each day his schedule includes contacting ten people from his existing relationship base. He calls them and typically leaves a voice mail just to say "hello." He always gives them permission not to return the call. He just wants them to know that they are on his mind — and to re-establish himself as a member of their relationship bases.

Ask Great Questions.

Ever notice that it's often the person in the room who is asking really good questions who is also the most revered? It's true. Next time you sit in on a Q&A session following a lecture or in a meeting, look closely and you'll see what I mean. I find, almost invariably, all eyes turn to the first person who asks a great question — with all minds thinking, "What a great question. Why didn't I ask it?"

The best example I can think of in terms of always coming up with slam dunk questions is NPR's Terry Gross, long-time host of the radio show "Fresh Air." She is a highly skilled interviewer and I am endlessly amazed at how she gets even her most reclusive, reserved guests to open up, or at how she elicits responses from guests you've heard interviewed a million times before on other broadcasts say things they've probably never before said publicly. I love how she probes and urges her visitors to go a layer deeper... then another layer deeper... then another. And, none of it sounds scripted. Oh, like any good interviewer, I'm sure she goes in prepared — knowing enough about her guest's interests, expertise, background, etc. so that she can engage with them, peer-to-peer, but that doesn't explain the magic — the interviews are so authentic, so real, so raw, so unlike any others. She seems to start the interview with one key question — and it's often one that seems offbeat — and then the rest of the conversation flows so organically. The listener usually learns something about the guest's upbringing, early career, passions. I suppose the best explanation for why all of her interviews sound so natural is, simply put, they are. She listens — really listens — to the guest's initial response, then asks the next logical question, one that is clearly prompted not by Terry's original script, but by the interviewee's response. Even those guests who seem reticent to respond come back with personal, thoughtful, thorough answers — when they don't, Terry asks another question to get them talking. And, hey, she's Terry Gross, so it stands to reason that perhaps she has some license to ask the more probing, more personal questions — we might not all have that type of authority — but paying careful attention to her style can be very instructive. There isn't anyone who couldn't learn a thing or two by listening to some of her interviews.

To become a master at the art of asking great questions, I advise you to listen, really listen; be genuinely curious; don't have a pre-determined list of questions that you feel you must get through; even if you do have a pre-determined list of questions, allow the answers to come organically and out of order; and more specifically, allow your questions to be iterative and organic based on the answer to the prior question. [117]

Coffee-Lunch-Coffee-Drinks.

For the truly savvy networkers, this tip is especially useful for successful holiday season networking. There is a time, during the weeks between Thanksgiving and New Year's Eve when the atmosphere out there changes. I don't know what it is. It's not just that it gets cooler outside or that the promise of snow becomes a reality. I don't think that it is really calendared, or that employers wish for it to happen, but work seems to slow to a rather snail-like pace. Okay, that may not be true in the retail world, but it certainly is for all office-based businesses, when people tend to turn their attention away from the hustle and bustle of work life and begin to feel "holiday cheer."

Let's set that aside for a moment. There is another phenomenon that happens among many job seekers. I've heard it too many times. The story line goes something like, "I'd like to find a new job, but, you know, nobody hires during the holiday season, so I think that I will just take off some time to relax and I will get back to my job search after the start of the year." You've heard it, too, right? But here's what I want to tell you about that: It's a mistake! Don't take your eyes off the prize now! The holiday season is actually a great time to get your name out there, to let people know what you are interested in doing and that you are serious.

Bringing all of this back together, here's the secret... seize the holiday season! Whether you are a job seeker, a sales person or simply a master networker, you can add a whole new dimension to your holiday cheer and increase your networking more than 30% by employing my seasonally-adjusted, super holiday networking tactic: **Coffee-Lunch-Coffee-DRINKS!**

I discovered this secret weapon of networking mastery several years ago. It turns out that many people are willing to break away from the standard work schedule between 4-4:30pm to meet YOU, my dear networker, for a glass of wine to toast the season! Don't like wine? No need to whine... go for a beer. Not the drinking type, you know by now that my beverage of choice is always a Coke®. If that doesn't work for you, go with the super fancy ice water with a lemon wedge. The point is, because office life does have a tendency to slow down and because working hours are often mysteriously replaced by office holiday parties and luncheons, it is within your power to finally get together with that awesome contact you have long wanted to meet or have had trouble connecting with by suggesting one of four different times to meet during the day vs. the normal three that I personally tout.

And, given the holiday cheer component of my message, it might be a particularly good time to re-connect with someone with whom you have lost touch or have been thinking about but simply haven't had the chance to catch up with in some time. Go for it! They almost certainly have been wishing to catch up with you, too.

Reconnect.

Think back — to grade school, your youth sports league, college, maybe your first job… with whom would you love to reconnect? Or, was there someone who you were not necessarily close with, but whom you are curious about? Reach out. Reconnect.

I recently reconnected with Rick, a guy with whom I went to high school. Though we haven't seen much of each other in more than twenty years, it turns out we are now in complementary lines of business. He helps sales professionals become more successful and I help entrepreneurs to start and grow companies. All entrepreneurs must possess strong sales skills — all sales people must think entrepreneurially. You get the idea. Rick and I had much to discuss and information to exchange. There was great value to reconnecting and I'm so glad we did.

A woman named Sara Nelson, who is a friend of my editor, Leigh Haber, tells this story: Sara recently moved from one great job to another, becoming Editorial Director for Amazon, where she is responsible [119] for a redesign of their books page and for "curating" editors' picks for readers. How did she get the job, besides that she has also been Books Editor for *O Magazine* and the editor-in-chief for *Publisher's Weekly*, which is the book industry's go-to trade magazine? She has great contacts among top-ranking executives, but her very smart tip is that:

> *"People think they should network up but I've actually found that befriending and staying in touch with people who were once junior to me opens up all sorts of avenues as time goes on, and they get more senior. My former editorial assistant (18 years my junior) eventually grew into the job I left (at* Self Magazine*) when I moved on. We stayed in touch and now she's much more senior than I am, (but on a slightly different track from mine). She got herself a job at Amazon and is one of the people who recommended me for my job there."*

Just as Tom Peters observed, which was cited earlier in the book, it's certainly not about "sucking up."

Networking Groups.

Once you have mastered all the types of interactions we've already described, what else remains? For executives, company founders, presidents of organizations, a few other options are available. Many choose to join more exclusive types of membership organizations. By those I am not necessarily referring to country clubs, social clubs or golf clubs, although these can be excellent ways to connect, but rather, to smaller, more intimate networking groups that exist all over the country; and, in fact, all over the world.

One example is Business Networking International or BNI. Let me open by saying this is not a sales pitch — I do not belong to a BNI group, though I do know several people who do, and who enjoy what BNI has to offer. According to the BNI website (bni.com), the organization boasts more than 145,000 members internationally, and bills itself as the largest business networking and referral marketing organization in the world. My understanding of the way these chapters work is that a diverse group of professionals are invited to join — there can be no more than one of each "type" of professional, e.g. one financial planner, one marketer, one attorney, et al. per chapter. Again, per the organization's own marketing, in 2011, BNI generated 6.9 million referrals resulting in $3.1 billion dollars' worth of business for its members. Not bad for a year's work!

Another example is Vistage (vistage.com). Like BNI, Vistage, a 15,000 member organization, creates small, intimate groups of professionals who join by invitation only. These exclusive CEO peer advisory groups meet regularly and ensure that members receive the coaching and guidance they necessary to address challenging workplace issues. I am not a member of Vistage, but know several highly successful individuals who participate in Vistage groups. Both BNI and Vistage are pay-to-play organizations, by the way.

For my own purposes, I helped to organize my own professional peer group under the leadership of my friend, Neil Schwartz, vice president at Cerner Corporation. Neil and I gathered together a small group of professionals and met formally each month for a year covering topics that would help us to expand our skill sets, enhance our individual decision-making capabilities, provide unlimited learning, improve our performance and encourage a sense of ownership within our community. We brought in guest speakers, engaged in intense, detailed discussion, worked on special projects together and came to rely on one another for guidance, peer mentorship and advice for tough subjects and issues we each faced in the workplace. Though it has been some time since we held our formal meetings, without exception, I continue to count on these individuals — and they on me — as we progress in our careers.

So, of course, the moral of this story is: PRACTICE, PRACTICE, PRACTICE! It turns out that practice (for about 10,000 hours) makes "expert," though there is no such thing as "perfect," which means — practice is for life. So get out there, NOW! and start networking. Start clocking those hours.

In the course of researching and writing this book, and in composing my blog posts, I have had the unparalleled opportunity to read the words of some of the greatest connectors of our time, or to listen to their words via speeches, interviews, or sometimes, in person, one-on-one. So as a kind of parting gift from me (from them) to you, here are some of the top takeaways I have gleaned from my experiences and interactions, tools that master networkers use every day:

1. *When you receive a referral,*
   always follow up in a timely fashion.

   This keeps the referral fresh in your mind, and is both the polite and efficient thing to do. You never know what will come of a new referral — it's really a new opportunity.

2. *Your reputation is all you've got.*

   Be trustworthy. Earn the trust of those in your network and don't let them down.

3. *Stay positive.*

There is enough doom and gloom out there. With calmness and confidence, present yourself to the world as a person who knows themselves and knows the score; and, therefore, knows enough to know that after the darkness comes the light.

4. *Be helpful.*

Always keep your ear to the ground for opportunities that will be useful to others in your network. That is really what connectivity is all about.

5. *Develop your listening skills.*

There is enough noise out there. You don't have to be part of the din. Practice active listening by purposefully focusing on the person speaking with you.

6. *Be grateful.*

If you have a network, you have a safety net. You have colleagues. You have friends. What could be better than that?

7. *Stay on duty at all times.*

A friend of mine recently met an important new contact on a short flight from one airport to another during her vacation. A friendly conversation led to a great new opportunity. You never know.

8. *Be truly sincere.*

Even if the person on the other end of the phone can't see what you're doing, give them your full attention. Don't multi-task while talking to someone. Put away your cell phone. Stop browsing emails or surfing the web. Be present.

9. *Be the most enthusiastic and motivated person in the room.*

Those are the people who invariably land the clients or the jobs. Do your homework. Learn your subject. And project that enthusiasm.

10. *Become an expert at working your network.*

Use contact management software to maintain your contact database. Organize your email addresses. Carry your business cards as well as those of your referral partners with you. Exude mastery.

Networking.

By now you've read the word so many times it may be making you dizzy. And as I reflect on the advice I've offered, I also think about what really inspires me, what really feeds me, what keeps me going from one day to the next. The fuel that keeps my networking engine in top working order has nothing to do with being a whirling dervish, spinning from one meeting to another, madly dashing off from one coffee meeting, to a lunch meeting, to a third meeting in a day. There is an underlying rhythm in my life that always keeps me grounded, and that keeps me focused on what's really important. My core network, which consists of the people and things closest to me, whose well-being is so closely tied to my own, is my center. Without that center, there would be no extended network. Without that core, I would be running from here to there, without an underlying purpose. My purpose is meaningful connection, within myself, within my family, within my community, within my professional and social network — in the world. With purpose, with the strength that comes from being able to depend on one's core, true engagement, true connection, can happen every day. It's what makes life worth living.

Relationships Work Kansas City Friendship Everything Goals Inspiration Sports Family Competition Fun Cinema Love Photography Faith Coffee Lunch Coffee Nature Entrepreneurship Literature NYC Energy Travel NETWORKING Music Life Colleagues Theatre Food People Connections

AFTERWORD

Writing this book has been like participating in a real, live networking experiment. Knowing that I was creating my blog, with an eye towards eventually becoming enough of a master networker to be ready to share what I'd learned with you, in the form of a book, amplified all of the networking possibilities around me. What's really powerful about that, when you stop to think about it, is that when we are open to connection, we realize that every human being has a story to tell, that that story may have some real relevance for us, and that our experiences and knowledge may have value for them. Building and maintaining a network made up of people—who have had successes, failures, moments of despair and triumph—this brings us all closer, and makes the world feel a little bit more manageable.

It is easy to say to one's self: "It's who you know, and I have no way of knowing everyone. How can I possibly compete?" What you can do is this: Build your network, brick by brick, one contact at a time. Everyone has a choice when it comes to taking advantage of opportunities to connect with others. Your choice is clear. How are you going to proceed from here on out? Are you content to stay static, to leave your fate to "the fates," or are you going to take matters into your own hands, today, right now, and connect? My recommendation: Let's Connect!"

Alana

✉ Alana@coffeelunchcoffee.com

🌐 CoffeeLunchCoffee.com

🐦 @alanamuller #clcConnect

f facebook.com/coffeelunchcoffee

in linkedin.com/in/alanamuller

About the Author

Alana Muller is President of Kauffman FastTrac®, a global provider of training to aspiring and existing entrepreneurs — giving them the tools, resources and networks to start and grow successful businesses. Kauffman FastTrac® was created by the Kauffman Foundation, the largest foundation whose mission is to advance entrepreneurship as a key to growing economies and expanding human welfare.

Alana has a master's degree in business administration from the University of Chicago, where she was the recipient of the Mike and Karen Herman Family Fellowship for Women in Entrepreneurship, and an undergraduate degree in mathematics from Smith College. She was recognized as a 2012 Influential Woman by *KC Business* magazine.

Additionally, Alana is a member of the advisory boards of Morningstar Communications and the Blue Valley Center for Advanced Professional Studies and is actively involved in the community, serving on several not-for-profit boards including those of the Jewish Community Center, the Jewish Community Foundation, Women's Division of the Jewish Federation of Greater Kansas City, the American Heart Association's Go Red for Women and the Smith College Alumnae Association of Greater Kansas City. She and her husband, Marc Hammer, live in Overland Park, Kansas, with their son, Ian, and their dog, Cinco.

Connect with Alana at Alana@coffeelunchcoffee.com.

Check out her blog at CoffeeLunchCoffee.com.

And follow her on Twitter @alanamuller #clcConnect.

CPSIA information can be obtained at www.ICGtesting.com
Printed in the USA
LVOW07s2104200814

400111LV00010B/163/P